# SAVORY STEWS

"There are only two ingredients essential to the making of a good stew: time and love. Everything else that goes into the pot will vary in accordance with taste, availability and budget. Technically, to stew is to simmer—and you can simmer almost anything: beef bones, lobster claws, morsels of lamb, old hens, rabbits, beans, pigs' knuckles . . . a more detailed list will be found in the Index . . ."

Here are recipes for plain and fancy stews, stews for beginners *and* for gourmets, stews from around the block *and* from around the world. It may well become the *most used* book you own.

# SAVORY STEWS

by
## Mary Savage

**MODERN PROMOTIONS/PUBLISHERS**
A Division of Unisystems, Inc. New York, New York 10022

Printed in Canada

# ACKNOWLEDGMENTS

Enough recipes to fill a cookbook are hard to come by. I am indebted to people all over the country for taking the trouble to write down and send me the recipes for their favorite stews. Specifically, my thanks as follows (and my apologies if I have omitted anyone):

To Anniel Bishop for "Beef Stew with Wine and Brandy"; Bill Boggess for "Texas Chili Beans"; Eleanor Coates for "Beef à la Stroganoff" and "Economy Beef with Beer"; Lee Cox for "Chinese Pot Roast Chicken" and "Old-Fashioned Beef Stew"; Lillian De La Torre for "Chicken in Brandy and Cream"; Harrison Doyle for "Covered Wagon Stew with Marrow Dumplings"; De Forbes for "Company Beef Stew"; Jo Gottsdanker for "Economy Hungarian Stew," "Lamb Ragout" and "Boiled Beef"; Sheila Lynds for "Shrimp and Artichoke Stew"; Eunice Montgomery for "Stewed Swiss Steak"; Anne Pidgeon for "Lamb Stew with Artichoke Hearts" and "Filipino Marinated Chicken and Pork"; Esse Raffelock for "Chicken Stewed in Orange Sauce" and "Veal Stewed in Red Wine"; Tommy Reagon for "Pot Roast with Beer" and "Mulligan Stew with Tomatoes"; Bill Richardson for "Venison Chili"; Ming Sedacca for "Spiced Pot Roast"; and Margaret Warsavage for "Pork Kidney Stew."

# CONTENTS

# INTRODUCTION

## *What Is a Stew?*

THERE ARE only two ingredients essential to the making of a good stew: time and love. Everything else that goes into the pot will vary in accordance with taste, availability and budget. Technically, to stew is to simmer—and you can simmer almost anything: beef bones, lobster claws, morsels of lamb, old hens, rabbits, beans, pigs' knuckles . . . a more detailed list will be found in the Index, but even it won't be complete, inasmuch as certain stewable items, such as iguanas, have had to be omitted from this book because of the author's lack of experience with them.

Whatever you simmer, the simmering is the thing. That's where the time comes in. A stew is a slow developer, and should never be hastened. It needs only the very tiniest amount of heat, just enough to cause barely discernible bubbles to rise to the surface at a leisurely pace. Left to its own devices, it will then meld, marry and grow toothsome.

But don't leave it to its own devices for too long or it will grow mushy. The very best stews are those that are cocked one day, refrigerated overnight and then reheated for serving. That session in the refrigerator contributes a certain mellowness and wisdom that fresh, new stews simply do not have.

The difficulty is to sneak the stew into the refrigerator before anyone gets a whiff of the delectable odors that are rising from it. Even the cook must be a person of the most rigorous self-denial in order to resist the temptation to taste too much, lest the "taste" become a bowlful and the bowlful a succession of servings for spouse, children and neighbors, after which there will be so little stew left that you might as well finish it.

The second essential ingredient for a stew is love. Love is what decides upon the companions you provide for the beef ribs, ham hocks, oysters or whatever it is that is being simmered. These include an enormous variety of items. Vegetables are most common, but fruits or nuts are also used, and the full range of herbs and spices. Poetry surely has been written about the bouquet garni, that fragrant assortment of fresh herbs and spices bound in a small cheesecloth bag and dropped into the stew to cook just long enough to give the stew a sense of its own identity.

Also, many stews include a starch, such as barley, rice, potatoes or macaroni. These products work as thickening agents and also give your stew greater body and a longer life, an important consideration if the stew must feed a great many very hungry people (such as one fourteen-year-old boy I know). Other stews use more discreet thickeners, such as flour or cornstarch or tomato paste or arrowroot.

And then there is the matter of the liquid in which you do your simmering. You can use water if you have to, but almost anything else is better: milk, beer, wine, broth. Sometimes it is necessary to make two stews in order to end up with one good one. First, you stew some bones, together with an onion, a bay leaf, a carrot and some peppercorns, in water, and then you use the resulting liquid in the stew you are going to serve.

And there you have it: a bit of meat or fish or poultry, some fresh garden vegetables, a generous amount of broth, a few of your favorite herbs. Inform it with love and give it lots of time to develop, and you will be rewarded with a fine and handsome stew.

10

Fine and handsome stews come in many disguises. Consider, for example, the following case in point.

Once upon a time an impoverished Frenchman spotted an old, unlicensed rooster wandering down the street all by its lonesome, and, driven by hunger, he seized it, wrung its neck, stripped and gutted it and threw it into a stewpot. He then added a bottle or two of whatever red wine he happened to have on hand (everyone knows that French cellars are chockablock full of vintage wines) and a handful of herbs, and let the thing simmer over very low heat for a day and a half, at the end of which time he had—you guessed it—coq au vin.

Or take the Russian who cut a chunk of beef into strips, simmered it for a while, added sour cream and tomato sauce to give the world beef à la Stroganoff. And then there are the Italians with their chicken cacciatore and the Spanish with mustacholi and the Germans with sauerbraten. There are stews made with curry powder and stews made with chili powder and stews made with peanut butter, each quite common in its own part of the world. And who doesn't know about Hungarian goulash or the heartiest broth of them all— plain old Irish stew?

In short, stews are truly international. The merest peek behind the fancy name and you will discover what you suspected all along: that it's a stew.

Back in the days when our rugged ancestors were catching their meals on the hoof, they discovered that a cooked dinner was not only more flavorful, but also easier to eat. The customary method of cooking was direct application of heat to the edible object, a process which anyone who has chewed his way through the foods proffered at a modern outdoor barbecue will recognize as primitive and uncivilized. There ought to be a statue raised to that first great lady of yore who conceived the notion of putting a receptacle between the heat and the meat, thereby giving her control of the amount and distribution of cooking temperature.

When our heroine threw those mastodon toes or wild horse shanks or whatever into a potful of hot water for a couple of hours, she really started something. Whether she told her neighbors who told their neighbors who told their neighbors, or whether the neighbors all accomplished the same trick at the same time doesn't matter: The word got around, and today every people has its own stew that is as special to it as its language or its folk costume. The dish may be made out of rabbit and called hasenpfeffer, but it's still a stew.

The problem is one of definition. One would like to say simply that a stew is a stew is a stew, but, alas, there are those who do not find this sort of thing satisfactory.

Nevertheless, setting boundaries for stew-making is not easy. A pot roast cooked on top of the stove with gravy and vegetables is a stew, but a potful of meat and vegetables and gravy cooked in the oven is usually called a casserole. A stew in which all of the liquid is absorbed by rice is no longer a stew, but a pilaf or a pilau or a paella, depending upon the part of the world in which it is made. Sometimes it is even called arroz con pollo.

The distinction between a soup and a stew is a fine one, the full discussion of which should probably be given over to a Ph.D. thesis. However, if you think it over, you will realize that it is as simple as most complicated things, to wit: A soup can be drunk, but a stew must be eaten with a utensil of some sort.

When I began collecting material for this cookbook, I asked my friends to send me recipes for their favorite stews, and some of the responses I received went like this:

"But I don't have a *decent* stew." (I replied that I would love to have the recipe for an indecent stew, as that would surely put my book on the best-seller list.)

"But I never measure for a stew; I don't know what I put in it."

"I never make the same stew twice; I just use whatever's handy."

Or, as one friend put it: "Is there more than one?"

In short, although everyone made stews, very few knew how they did it. Moreover, the attitude was frequently that stews are second-class food, not to be discussed in polite company.

Such points of view are to be deplored. In the first place, a nice balance of flavors deserves to be repeated —obviously impossible if you don't know what it is you are repeating.

In the second place, a good stew is not a catchall for the week's leftovers, except in those instances in which they clamor to be combined. A stew deserves the best you can bring to it (time and love, remember?), no matter how inexpensive or unpretentious the ingredients.

A successful stew is just as fine an example of the culinary art as a successful soufflé, perhaps more so. For one thing, most stews involve two processes which can be tricky: sautéing and braising. No less an authority than Escoffier says so. Meat cut in chunks is lightly browned (sautéed) in hot fat and then braised in a sauce. And that is stewing.

Thus, if you are inclined to have an inferiority complex about stews, or if your family sneers at them, here's what you do. When the question of what's for dinner arises, don't say, "beef stew," say, "braised beef with vegetables." Or, if you really want to be fancy, say, "Beef sauté braised in sauce de la maison."

Remember that kings, princes, presidents and dictators have thrived on stews and lent their names to them. If you had any pioneer forefathers, they never would have made it long enough to beget those who begot you without the stew. That little old log cabin had a stewpot going all of the time, and the most sought-after women were not the prettiest, but the best stew-makers. When you, in your comparatively sophisticated kitchen, put together a stew, you are carrying forward a proud tradition.

The reason stews have been and are so important is, of course, that they are nutritious. All of the goodness of the meat and vegetables is incorporated in the broth or sauce, instead of being lost, as is the case in so many other cooking processes. A bowlful of stew is not only wonderfully tasty and satisfying, but it is also chockablock full of all of those mysterious, invisible somethings that provide energy, stamina and stability. A stew is usually a complete meal in itself; all it needs for perfection is a bottle of wine and a tossed green salad.

In this harried, hurried age, it is well to remember that stews are great timesavers. The time required for cooking a stew is its own, not yours. All you have to do is start it, and then you can go and play bridge or pull weeds or take a nap or go to the races. Furthermore, a stew is usually good for two, three or even four meals; it can be stored for short periods in the refrigerator or it can be frozen. Reheating it can be done while you're at the hairdresser or making fancy hors d'oeuvres or reading a book. Whatever you do, you can do it with the assurance that time is being saved all over the place.

Finally, there is the flexibility of stews. Whether it's elegance or economy you're after, there is a stew admirably suited for the occasion. There are dinner-party stews and stews to stretch the budget until payday. There are busy-day stews and stews for long and lazy afternoons. Some cuts of meat are suitable only for stewing, and there is but one thing you can do with a stewing hen. On the other hand, stews can be costly and the results can be sumptuous, but the two things are not necessarily synonymous.

## In Practice . . . A Few Hints

WHEN you set out to make a stew, there are certain basic utensils required; there are also a few hints that will make your stew-cooking activities more successful.

First, and most important, is the pot. A good stewpot is about the most practical piece of kitchen equipment you can own. It should be heavy (cast aluminum or cast iron, for example), big (four quarts minimum) and have a snug-fitting cover. Such a pot is essential for soups and sauces as well as stews; it's great for boiling potatoes and other vegetables, or spaghetti and other pastas; you can sauté in it or use it as a deep-fat fryer, and if you get one that has nonflammable knobs or handles, you can put it in the oven. And a good-looking stewpot can be your serving dish, too!

Along with the pot, you should have at least one large spoon with a long handle. Two spoons are even better (a solid one and one with holes in it, so that you can lift the meat or fish or whatever out of the broth). You may want a long-handled fork, too, for poking and pushing, but don't use it for piercing, as this lets all kinds of good juices run out, leaving the merest residue of what was formerly a tasty morsel. This is particularly important with chicken and with meats that are floured and seared, as the purpose of the searing is to seal in the juices.

You should make it an absolute rule never to put anything in your stewpot that you would not care to eat or drink all by its lonesome. You'll end up with a witch's brew, and it will be all that you deserve. A stew is not the place to get rid of limp vegetables or stringy meat; feed the former to the rabbit and the latter to the dog, or, lacking these conveniences, toss them both into the garbage disposal.

The foregoing rule applies especially to wines in

15

stews. A stew is only as good as its parts, and many an otherwise excellent stew has been ruined by the addition of cheap wine or so-called "cooking sherry." If a stew deserves wine, it deserves good wine. Many of the recipes in this cookbook call for sake, which my husband and I use, as it is both inexpensive and drinkable. If you don't care for sake or can't get it, substitute any good table wine or sherry, but dilute the sherry half and half with water.

If you are a true devotee of the culinary art, you will make your own broths from scratch, a process which requires even more time and love than stew-making. However, there are so many packaged products available commercially today, generally of good quality, that, with a pinch of this and a sniff of that, you can create an excellent broth in no time (well, almost). My husband, who is a superb stew-maker and rather old-fashioned in clinging to the long, hard way of doing things, frequently uses one of the dry-soup mixes as a beginning ingredient of a stew. One thing of which to be wary if you follow this procedure is the amount of salt added. Dry-soup mixes and condensed broths are quite adequately salted to start with, and I know of no efficient way to remedy an oversalted stew. You can add water, but this will thin your brew and throw its proportions out of balance, so that you will spend the rest of the day or night making adjustments, much like the fellow trying to even up the table legs.

On the other hand, there are several things that you can save which will enrich the flavor of your stews. Mushroom stems, for example, can be tossed into the stew for an hour or so and then removed; you wouldn't want to try to eat them, as they tend to be tough. Or, if you are simmering mushrooms for any reason, save the liquor; it's a great substitute for plain water.

We always save gravies and sauces at our house, even if there's only a tablespoonful. You never know when that particular tablespoonful will be the ingre-

16

dient that converts your stew into a masterpiece. Of course, if you make a stew only once a year, your refrigerator will get pretty well cluttered up, but, in that case, you either don't need this cookbook at all, or you need it desperately.

Court bouillon should always be saved. That's the broth that results from cooking vegetables or fish, but usually it refers to fish. Frequently, it is made as a normal part of the preparation of a fish stew, but there are other times when you might find yourself with a court bouillon on your hands for which you have no immediate use, when you have cooked shrimp or lobster or crab, say, which you intend serving without further ado. You will have cooked your shellfish in a liquid composed of wine and water, with maybe a dash of lemon juice, some peppercorns, a slice of onion, half a carrot and a bay leaf, and it would be wicked to throw the resulting broth away. Make a vow that you will prepare a fish stew in the near future, and strain the liquid into a jar for future reference. This is one broth you have to make yourself; I have never seen it in a can on a supermarket shelf.

When it comes to thickening, the new instant flours are marvelous for achieving the right consistency at the end of the cooking period. However, it has been my experience that they should be handled much as you handle cornstarch or potato flour, i.e., they should be stirred into the liquid slowly, with the pot *off the fire*. If you toss a handful of instant flour into a cheerfully bubbling stew, the result will be lumps, and there simply won't be anything you can do about them.

One final word. The recipes in this cookbook are not guaranteed, because some people are constitutionally unable to follow a recipe the way it is given, and others are unable to read in the kitchen. I belong to the latter category, and once tried to cook two pounds of shrimp in half a cup of champagne, when the recipe clearly instructed me to use half a *bottle* of champagne.

However, every recipe in this cookbook has been tested in my own kitchen and written down in such a way that I hope it will work in yours. My kitchen, I might add, is an ordinary, next-door-neighbor type kitchen, somewhat cluttered and sometimes chaotic, due to the presence of two hungry dogs, two inquisitive cats, and a small child who is always playing drums with the stewpot just when I need it.

My husband and I frequently cook together, and most of these recipes were created and tested as joint endeavors. We hope that anyone who uses this cookbook will have as much fun and enjoyment with stews as we have.

*Mary Savage*

# 1

## THE COW, THE CALF,
## THE LAMB AND THE PIG

### (Meat Stews)

IN THESE days of attrition of personal services, it is as difficult to find a good butcher as it is to find a good piano tuner or a good blacksmith (provided you can find any at all). The old-fashioned butcher shop, where your meat was cut the way you wanted it and where, in the process of shopping, you were necessarily educated as to how various cuts of meat should appear, has been replaced by yards and yards of gleaming chromium refrigerated tubs filled with tidy parcels of meat enclosed in various kinds of plastic. (It has been my experience that all too often the meat tastes as if it were made of some kind of plastic, too.)

In the most modern supermarkets, one is permitted to observe the butchers at their work behind glass panels, much as one views new babies in the hospital nursery. These people are so frightfully busy with their measuring, slicing and packaging (what one might call the "dis-assembly line") that I, for one, am much too intimidated to push the button that would interrupt this display of efficiency. On the few occasions when I have dared to ask for service, I have been informed (rather happily, it seemed to me) that whatever it was I wanted was not available, usually because it hadn't "come in yet," but sometimes because it had "gone out," presumably having been sliced, chopped or ground up and wrapped in one of those little packages. No matter when I make my timid inquiry, it seems that I am there too early or too late.

If you are fortunate enough to deal with a real, live butcher, be nice to him, and he will not only help you to select the best tenderloin, but he will also guide you in the selection of stew meats.

The first thing to remember when you go out to buy some meat for a stew is to avoid anything marked "stew meat." Material so labeled invariably turns out to be cubes of solid, tough beef without an ounce of fat in a carload, and it is just as essential to have some fat in your stew meat as it is to have a properly marbled steak for broiling. For the most part, you will get best results from shanks, shoulder cuts and rib meat, as well as oxtails and neck bones. Some people, however, prefer chuck and round steak, and there are many recipes in this cookbook calling for these cuts, although, generally speaking, they require longer cooking and greater care to avoid dryness.

Perhaps one reason for the popularity of lean beef in stews is that it prevents the accumulation of fat, which makes any stew unattractive. If so, it is pretty silly, because disposing of excess fat is an extremely simple procedure. When the meat is almost cooked and before any vegetables are added, pour off the top of the stew liquid and place it in the freezing compartment of your refrigerator, where the fat will congeal on the top while the stew continues to cook. Or, if you are preparing the stew one day with the intention of serving it the next, the fat will congeal on top overnight in the refrigerator. In either case, all you have to do is skim it off with a fork or spoon and you have a lovely, fat-free broth to deal with.

To BEGIN WITH, here is a very basic stew, capable of infinite variation, as your imagination and refrigerator contents warrant. It is hearty and nourishing, and if you don't eat all of it the first night, you can freeze what's left and serve it a week from Thursday.

## BASIC BEEF STEW

*3 to 4 pounds beef shoulder, cut into 1½-inch cubes*
*1 cup flour*
*1 tablespoon seasoned salt*
*3 tablespoons bacon drippings or other fat*
*2 to 3 quarts water*
*2 packages dry onion soup mix*
*2 large cloves garlic, minced*
*6 stalks celery, diced*
*2 large onions, sliced*
*¾ cup uncooked barley*
*2 green peppers, cored and quartered*
*2 bunches small carrots, scraped and quartered*

Have your butcher cube the meat. Put flour and seasoned salt in a paper bag and add meat, shaking well to coat all sides. Put fat into your stewpot over a hot fire. More fat may be added if necessary, but try to end up with all the fat absorbed by the floured meat. Sear the meat on all sides in two or three batches. Return all seared meat to pot and add at least 2 quarts of water and bring to a light boil. Stir in onion soup mix, add the garlic, celery, onions and barley, and reduce the heat so the liquid barely simmers. Cover and cook at least 2 hours, or until meat is fairly tender, adding water if needed. If there is more fat than you like, pour 1 or 2 cups of the gravy off the top and place in freezing compartment of refrigerator. At the same time, add green peppers and carrots and continue to simmer until vegetables are tender—about 45 minutes. Lift congealed fat off liquid from freezer and discard. Return liquid to pot, heat and serve. *Makes 8 to 10 servings.*

IF YOU have ever cooked a stew of any kind, anywhere, anyhow, it was probably a "mulligan stew," which is a "stew made of any available meats or vegetables," according to the *Dictionary of American Slang*. Just what the origin of this word might be is obscure. One would like to attribute it to a person named Mulligan, but I have been unable to establish that such a person ever existed, or, if he did, that he ever made a stew. It is more likely one of those words that seeps into the language from unknown sources, like water working its way out of the ground. It may have originated with the hoboes of another era, a colorful lot who sat around their stewpots of an evening, inventing words and references that would one day become a part of our language. Whatever its origin, a mulligan stew is as good as its ingredients, and here are two for your delectation.

## MULLIGAN STEW WITH CREAMED CORN

2  *pounds beef shoulder, cut into 2-inch cubes*
3  *10½-ounce cans condensed beef bouillon*
1  *quart water*
*Seasoned salt to taste*
*Pepper to taste*
1  *green pepper, cored and quartered*
1  *bunch small carrots, scraped and halved*
1  *medium head cauliflower, broken into small pieces*
½  *teaspoon marjoram*
½  *teaspoon thyme*
2  *1-pound, 1-ounce cans creamed corn*

Have your butcher cube the roast. Toss the meat into your stewpot together with bouillon and water. Bring to a simmer, and add seasoned salt and pepper to taste. Cover and simmer at least 2 hours, until meat is tender. Add green pepper, carrots and cauliflower, and cook

30 to 45 minutes, until vegetables are tender. Add herbs and corn. Cook about 10 minutes, stirring from bottom now and then to prevent corn from sticking. *Makes 6 to 8 servings.*

## MULLIGAN STEW WITH TOMATOES

2½  pounds chuck steak, cubed
1½  pounds beef shin or soup bones, cut into pieces
1  tablespoon salt
5  quarts water
½  cup uncooked barley
2  tomatoes, peeled, or 1 15-ounce can, drained
6  carrots, sliced
1  bunch celery, coarsely chopped with leaves
4  medium onions, sliced
2  cups whole-kernel corn, or 1 10-ounce package, frozen
2  cups green lima beans, or 1 10-ounce package, frozen
1  15-ounce can greens (collard, turnip or mustard)

Trim all fat from meat and put into heavy frying pan over high heat to render out the fat. Strain the fat and return to frying pan. Sear meat and bones on all sides, and reserve fat (you'll need it later). Place meat and bones in stewpot and add salt and water. Cover and simmer 2 hours. Remove meat and bones and strain broth back into pot. Add barley and tomatoes and simmer 1 hour. Add carrots and celery and simmer 15 minutes. Add onions and simmer 20 minutes. Heat corn, lima beans and greens in frying pan with meat fat about 10 minutes. Bone the meat and add to pot with the cooked greens and corn. Simmer very gently for another hour, stirring occasionally. *Makes 12 to 16 servings.*

ONE of the ways to transform an everyday family stew into a Sunday company stew is to substitute wine for water. Actually, as is the case with most things in this life, the process is a little more complicated than straight substitution. In the first place, if you use 100 per cent wine for your stewing liquid, the taste of the wine is likely to overpower everything else in the stew, with the possible exception of the garlic. So don't get too enthusiastic when you have that wine bottle in your hand.

In the second place, not just any old wine will do. Wine is not going to improve with cooking, so you should use in your stew the same wine that you intend to serve at the table later. If you think you are being economical by using inexpensive "cooking" wine, you are mistaken; what you are doing is degrading the quality of your stew. Look at it this way: You won't use very much of the bottle in the stew; what you don't use, you will drink; what you are going to drink had better be palatable. Anyhow, here is the first of many stew recipes made with wine.

## BEEF STEW WITH WINE

*1 cup flour*
*1 tablespoon seasoned salt*
*2½ pounds boned beef shoulder or neck meat, cubed*
*½ pound salt pork, washed and cubed*
*15 small onions, whole, peeled*
*12 to 16 carrots (depending on size), scraped and whole*
*Salt to taste*
*½ teaspoon freshly ground black pepper*
*1 small clove garlic, minced*
*½ teaspoon fines herbes\**

---

\* You can buy this ready-made, or you can make it yourself, using finely chopped parsley, tarragon, chives and chervil, with maybe a little thyme for good measure.

24

*4 cups dry red wine*
*Water to cover*
*2 cups fresh mushrooms, quartered, or*
*2 4-ounce cans mushrooms, drained*
*2 green peppers, cored and thinly sliced*

Put flour and seasoned salt in a paper bag and shake the meat cubes to coat thoroughly. Wash excess salt from salt pork and then drop it into your stewpot over high heat and cook (without letting it smoke) until cubes are dark brown. Remove from pot and reserve. Sear the meat cubes in the fat from the salt pork and remove from pot. Add onions and carrots to the hot grease and reduce heat. Sauté for 10 minutes. Return meat and salt pork to pot. Add seasonings and wine and enough water to cover well. Be very careful about adding salt, because some salt pork is much saltier than others. Cover and simmer at least 2 hours, until meat is quite tender. Pour off top half of liquid and place in freezing compartment to congeal the fat. Add water to stew if needed and throw in mushrooms. Cook for 30 minutes. Add green peppers and cook no more than 5 minutes longer. Remove congealed fat from liquid in freezer and discard. Return liquid to pot. Reheat and serve. *Makes 8 to 10 servings.*

THE FOLLOWING stew goes a step farther and uses wine *and* brandy. It is a real mouth-watering, heart-warming dish that profits not only from the luscious liquors used, but also from the offbeat (for stews) flavor of yams: Don't let the combination of ingredients frighten you— it's delicious!

### BEEF STEW WITH WINE AND BRANDY

*2 slices bacon*
*4 tablespoons butter*

⅓ cup flour
2 teaspoons salt
½ teaspoon pepper
3 pounds bottom round steak cut into 1-inch cubes
3 tablespoons good brandy
2½ cups dry red wine
3 sprigs parsley, chopped
3 bay leaves
¼ teaspoon thyme
2 cloves garlic, minced or pressed
4 medium yams
1 pound onions, chopped
½ pound mushrooms, sliced

Cook the bacon in stewpot and remove. Add butter. Put flour, salt and pepper in paper bag and add beef cubes. Shake to coat thoroughly. Sear the beef on all sides in fat. If excess fat remains, sprinkle seasoned flour from the sack until it is absorbed. Add bacon, brandy, wine, parsley, bay leaves, thyme and garlic, with water to cover if needed. (You can put the parsley, bay leaves, thyme and garlic into a small cheesecloth bag tied with string; that's a bouquet garni and can be removed from the stew before serving.) Cover and simmer for at least 2 hours, until meat is tender. Peel and slice yams into ½-inch slices and add. Add peeled and chopped onions. Add washed and sliced mushrooms. Simmer for about 20 minutes, until yams are tender. *Makes 10 to 12 servings.*

THOSE PIONEERS who opened up the western half of the United States for settlers, slaughtering Indians and buffalo as they went, lived on stews as mentioned heretofore. What went into the stew was whatever wildlife was handy, including, of course, the buffalo. The following recipe goes back to the 1850s and came to us from a friend, who got it from his grandmother, who crossed the plains in a covered wagon when she was fifteen. The original recipe called for buffalo shanks, which are a little difficult to come by these days, but beef shanks work just as well. You will notice that those pioneers didn't waste anything—this stew uses the meat, the bones *and* the marrow.

## COVERED WAGON STEW WITH MARROW DUMPLINGS

*3 pounds beef shank bones, with meat still on*
*1 large onion, sliced*
*2 carrots, scraped and whole*
*1 turnip, peeled and quartered*
*2 potatoes, peeled and quartered*
*1 medium can tomatoes*

DUMPLINGS

*1 egg*
*Marrow*
*½ teaspoon salt*
*Flour, as needed*

Have your butcher cut the shank bones into 3-inch pieces and split them so the marrow can be removed. Scrape out marrow and cover bones with salted water and boil for about 1 hour. Add vegetables and continue cooking until they begin to be tender. Beat the egg and mash into the warmed marrow with a little salt. Add enough flour to enable you to roll the dumplings between your palms into balls the size of small walnuts. Drop marrow balls into boiling soup, cover and simmer about 45 minutes. The more dumplings you have, the better this dish is, though you should be warned that the marrow dumplings are very rich. *Makes 4 servings.*

THE BIG PROBLEM with short ribs is what to do with all that fat. There are two customary ways of handling it. One is to render out the fat by sautéing the short ribs for a long time and then pouring it off. The other is to remove the fat from the top of the stew before adding the vegetables. I prefer the latter method, as I never seem able to get rid of the fat by sautéing without drying out the meat in the process. The following recipe calls for beer, which seems a natural with short ribs, but if you want to splurge, try cooking it with dry red wine. Serve whichever liquid you use in the cooking as the beverage accompaniment to the meal and you have it made.

## SHORT RIBS OF BEEF IN BEER

*2 pounds short ribs of beef*
*½ cup flour*
*2 tablespoons butter*
*1½ teaspoons salt*
*¼ cup chopped onion*
*Dash Worcestershire sauce*
*1 cup beer*
*½ cup beef bouillon*
*4 medium-size potatoes*
*4 carrots*
*4 turnips*
*4 small onions*
*Salt and pepper to taste*

Dredge the short ribs in the flour and brown slowly on all sides in butter that has been melted in your stewpot. Add salt, onion, Worcestershire sauce and beer. Cover the pot and simmer slowly for 2 hours, or until tender. Skim the excess fat from the liquid and add beef bouillon. Then add the vegetables. Sprinkle with salt and pepper and cook for another hour, or until vegetables are tender. *Serves 4.*

BECAUSE short ribs have so much fat on them, you have to allow quite a lot of uncooked meat for each serving when planning the meal. We allow 1 pound per person, if there are no vegetables in the stew. The following recipe presents yet another method of disposing of the fat with which short ribs are so generously supplied. Essentially, you steam it out instead of simmering it out, and it works extremely well. The deviled ribs have a piquant flavor, which is a refreshing change.

## DEVILED SHORT RIBS OF BEEF

*4  pounds short ribs of beef*
*1  medium onion, sliced*
*1  bay leaf*
*½  teaspoon ginger*
*1½  tablespoons brown sugar*
*1  heaping teaspoon salt*
*¼  teaspoon black pepper*
*2  tablespoons lemon juice*
*¼  cup soy sauce*
*½  cup ketchup*
*½  cup water*
*More water, if needed*
*Instant flour*

Spread out short ribs in cold stewpot and set pot over moderately high heat. Brown ribs well on all sides and discard the fat. Cover pot and reduce heat to low and cook for an hour and 45 minutes. Pour off all grease again. Add onion and bay leaf and return to low heat. Mix ginger, brown sugar, salt and pepper together in small bowl, stir in lemon juice and then the soy sauce. Add to ribs. Mix ketchup and water together and add to pot. Cover and cook for at least half an hour, until meat is tender. Pour off cooking liquid to measure it, and add water to make 2 cups if needed. Discard bay leaf and shake instant flour into the liquid to make a thin sauce. Return to pot and bring to a light boil, stirring well, and serve immediately. *Serves 4 to 6.*

A POT ROAST is a stew made with one large piece of meat instead of a lot of small pieces. Traditionally, the method of preparing a pot roast is to sear the meat, add liquid, and simmer for a couple of hours. You can use almost any cut of meat for a pot roast; as is the case with stew meat, some fat in the meat will give you a more succulent result. The names given to these various cuts of meat seem to be a matter of regional preference. In California, a very popular steak is called a "New York cut," something I never encountered while living in New York. Consult your good friend the butcher, remembering that the closer the roast comes to filling your stewpot, the better the finished product will be.

## BASIC POT ROAST WITH VEGETABLES

2  *tablespoons flour*
½  *teaspoon seasoned salt*
3  *pounds beef roast*
2  *tablespoons bacon drippings or other fat*
½  *cup sake or dry white wine (not sherry)*
½  *cup water*
2  *onions, chopped*
1  *tablespoon soy sauce*
1  *bunch baby carrots, scraped, whole*
4  *medium turnips, quartered*
3  *medium potatoes (or yams), quartered*
1  *large can artichoke hearts (optional)*

Mix flour and seasoned salt and spread over entire surface of roast, rubbing it in. Put bacon drippings or other fat in stew-pot over high heat, and sear the roast well on all sides. Add sake or white wine and water, onions and soy sauce, and reduce heat to a very slow simmer. Cover and cook for at least 2 hours, until meat is tender, adding water from time to time if needed. Add vegetables and cook about 30 minutes, until all are tender. *Serves 6.*

SOME PEOPLE like to use beer in their cooking instead of water or wine, and, judiciously applied, it can provide a very pleasant, slightly tart flavor. However, it can be carried too far, as we once discovered from a cookbook which poured beer all over everything, including, as I recall, scrambled eggs. The final suggestion in that cookbook was to make percolated coffee with beer instead of water; we tried it, and it was so awful that we despaired of ever restoring our coffeepot, let alone our stomachs.

Anyhow, pot roast and beer are one of those natural combinations that is certain to be appetizing, whether you drink the beer or cook the pot roast in it, or both. Hence the following:

## POT ROAST WITH BEER

*Salt and pepper to taste*
*3 pounds chuck roast*
*2 tablespoons bacon drippings or other fat*
*2 12-ounce cans beer*
*2 tart apples or pears, halved and unpeeled, but*
  *cored*
*10 small carrots, scraped, whole*
*10 small onions, peeled, whole*
*3 turnips, quartered*
*3 medium potatoes, quartered*
*More beer if needed*

Rub salt and freshly ground black pepper all over the

roast. Put fat in stewpot over hot fire and sear roast on all sides. Add beer and bring to a boil, then reduce to simmer. Arrange the apple or pear halves on top of the roast with toothpicks and simmer, covered, for about 1 hour. Add the vegetables in layers all around the roast, and continue cooking about 30 minutes until vegetables are cooked  The meat should be tender, but pink in the middle. *Serves 6 to 8.*

Pot roast can also be cooked in wine and marinated in wine, and for recipes for these two processes, I refer you to Chapter 4, "Stews Around the World" and Chapter 7, "Special Stews for Guests."

I HAVE encountered some raised eyebrows as to whether swiss steak is properly classified as a stew or not. Frankly, I don't see how there can be any argument. The process of cooking swiss steak is stewing, with the single difference that the meat is cut into serving pieces instead of bite-size chunks. The following recipe is an easy dish to serve at an informal party, as you can cook the meat in the morning and then warm it up in the oven or on top of the stove just before serving. In fact, the flavor of the meat and gravy is improved by the reheating.

## STEWED SWISS STEAK

   2  *tablespoons flour*
   ½  *teaspoon seasoned salt*
   ¼  *teaspoon pepper*
   1  *large slice top round, ½ inch thick, cut into 4
      serving pieces*
   3  *tablespoons butter*
   2  *tablespoons flour*
   2  *or 3 cups hot water*
   1  *tablespoon instant onion soup mix*

Put flour, seasoned salt and pepper into paper bag and shake pieces of steak in this to coat evenly. Melt butter in stewpot and brown meat nicely on both sides. Remove meat. Add 2 tablespoons flour to the pot and a little more butter if needed to absorb all the flour. Let this brown before adding water to make a very light gravy. Add onion soup mix and return meat to gravy. Simmer for 1 hour or more, until meat is very tender. *Serves 4.*

BRAISING is what stewing is all about, although, strictly speaking, braised meat is cooked on top of a bed of vegetables, whereas, in stews, the vegetables are added later in the cooking process. In braised meats, the vegetables tend to get pretty pulpy by the time the meat is cooked. Moreover, all the good stuff from the vegetables, like flavor and vitamins, goes into the gravy, so that you aren't really wasting anything if you throw the vegetables away and serve a batch which has been cooked separately and for a shorter time. You will also note that braised meat is not seared first, for that tends to seal in the juices, and you want them out in the gravy.

## BRAISED BEEF

½  *teaspoon seasoned salt*
¼  *teaspoon pepper*
4  *pounds top round, sliced and cut into serving pieces*
¼  *pound fat salt pork, washed and cubed*
1  *cup sliced celery*
1½ *cups sliced carrots*
2  *medium turnips, diced*
½  *cup parsnips, diced*
12  *small white onions, peeled and whole*
1  *clove garlic, pressed or minced*

2  bay leaves
1  quart hot water

Sprinkle seasoned salt and pepper over meat. Put salt
pork in stewpot over medium heat, then add all the
vegetables and the garlic and bay leaves. Put meat on
top of vegetables, reduce heat to low and cover tightly.
Cook 20 minutes before adding water. Simmer very
slowly for at least 3 hours, turning the pieces of meat
occasionally and adding more hot water if needed.
Serve when meat is tender, with or without vegetables.
*Serves 8.*

I THINK that one of the nicest things anyone can set on
the dinner table is a lamb stew. For one thing, lamb is
generally tenderer and juicier than beef. For another,
lamb seems to enjoy being stewed (as do some hu-
mans) and is therefore almost foolproof. With cheaper
cuts of beef, you can end up with a stew in which the
meat is stringy and will remain so throughout all eter-
nity. But lamb gives a little and takes a little and ar-
rives on your table as plump and jolly as it was when
you started. Furthermore, although, in the form of
chops, lamb tends to be in a financial class which many
of us admire from a distance, good lamb stew meat,
while not cheap, is at least attainable. And any cut of
lamb is stewable.

## BASIC LAMB STEW WITH VEGETABLES

2½  pounds lamb shoulder, boned and cubed
3  tablespoons flour
½  teaspoon seasoned salt
Bacon drippings or other fat, if needed
1  cup sake or dry white wine
4  cups hot water
1  large onion, sliced

*Bouquet garni, consisting of 1 clove garlic, sliced, 10
   whole black peppercorns, sprig fresh thyme, fresh
   chervil and fresh parsley tied in cheesecloth bag*
*Salt to taste*
*8 small carrots, scraped and halved*
*2 medium potatoes, quartered*
*10 small white onions*
*4 tablespoons flour*
*Cooking fat, as needed*

Have your butcher cut the boned shoulder into 1-inch cubes. Remove any excess fat and put it in stewpot over medium heat. Put flour and seasoned salt into a paper bag and shake the meat in it to coat well. When the pieces of fat are well browned, remove from pot and reserve. Brown the flour-coated meat on all sides in the rendered fat, adding bacon drippings or other fat if needed. Remove any extra fat from pot and reserve. Add the sake, hot water, sliced onion and bouquet garni, and bring to a slow boil. Add salt to taste. Cover and simmer slowly for about 2 hours, until meat is fairly tender. Add vegetables and continue cooking about 30 minutes, until vegetables are tender. If you had extra fat from the pot, mix enough of it with the 4 tablespoons of flour to make a paste. If not, melt a little bacon drippings or other fat to make your paste. Stir this into the stew to thicken slightly. Simmer 5 more minutes. *Serves 6 to 8.*

MY HUSBAND is a professional writer; he is also partial to stew and is, in general, an extremely good cook. I don't know whether all writers like stews, but I do know that many writers are good cooks, probably because the learning years of a writer are usually long and lonely and impecunious. After years of writing for almost nothing and living mostly on stews to make ends meet, my husband created a detective character named

Michael Shayne, who is today rather well known among mystery buffs. Because the earnings from Shayne pay most of our household bills, we call our home "Shanty Shayne," and because the following stew is Shayne's creator's creation, it is named accordingly:

## LAMB STEW, SHANTY SHAYNE

3 *lamb shanks*
2 *slices lamb neck, about 2 inches thick*
1 *cup flour*
1 *teaspoon seasoned salt*
½ *teaspoon pepper*
5 *cups water, or more, to cover*
1 *package dry onion soup mix*
2 *large onions, sliced*
3 *stalks celery, with leaves, sliced*
1 *clove garlic, minced*
½ *cup uncooked barley*
2 *green peppers, cored and quartered*
1 *large bunch baby carrots, scraped and whole*
6 *small turnips, quartered*
1 *cup sake or dry white wine*

Have your butcher cut the shanks in four pieces, and quarter the neck pieces. Remove all outside fat with sharp knife and put in stewpot over medium heat. Reduce the fat to cracklings, remove and reserve. Put the flour and seasonings in a paper bag and shake meat in it to coat well. Brown the pieces of meat in hot lamb fat on all sides, removing well-browned pieces and adding others until all are brown. If there is unabsorbed fat still in the pot, add seasoned flour to absorb it all. Return meat and cracklings to pot and add water. Bring to hard boil and stir in soup mix, onions, celery, garlic, barley and green peppers. Cover and reduce heat to slow simmer for 1½ hours or more, until meat is nicely tender. Add carrots, turnips and sake or white wine, and cook about 30 minutes, until vegetables are tender. *Serves 6 to 8.*


I WAS TEMPTED to put the following stew among party dishes, as it is rather elegant, but finally opted in favor of a curry for the dinner-party-lamb stew. The lady who gave me the recipe below frequently serves it to guests; when she makes it for her family, she freezes half of it for future reference. Either way, you will probably make it one of your regularly served stews, as we have.

## LAMB STEW WITH ARTICHOKE HEARTS

*3  pounds boned leg of lamb, cubed*
*½  cup flour*
*1  teaspoon salt*
*½  teaspoon black pepper*
*⅓  cup butter*
*3  medium onions, chopped*
*1  teaspoon garlic salt*
*½  teaspoon paprika*
*½  teaspoon dried rosemary*
*2  tablespoons lemon juice*
*1½  cups water*
*2  10-ounce packages frozen artichoke hearts*

Have your butcher bone a small leg of lamb, trim off all fat and cut into 1-inch cubes. This should produce about 3 pounds of wonderfully succulent meat, but half a pound one way or the other is unimportant. Put flour, salt and pepper in a paper bag and shake lamb cubes in it to coat. Brown in butter in stewpot. Add onions, garlic salt, paprika, rosemary, lemon juice and water. Cover and simmer for 1 hour. Add artichoke hearts and cook another 30 minutes. *Serves 8.*

LAMB SHANKS are really mighty fine eating. If you haven't already discovered them, don't waste any time getting acquainted, for they are among the tastiest cuts of meat available. To get the full value, you must cook the meat on the bone and serve it that way, which means that lamb shanks should not be included on the menu when you are trying to impress somebody with your elegant table manners. On the other hand, if you cook the meat quite thoroughly, it will fall off the bone, and a little fast work in the kitchen with a sharp knife will give you a stew that looks as though it had never seen a bone in its life. You don't want it to taste that way, however.

### LAMB SHANKS STEWED IN RED WINE

4 *lamb shanks*
4 *tablespoons flour*
1 *teaspoon seasoned salt*
½ *teaspoon seasoned pepper*
6 *slices bacon, diced*
1 *medium can tomatoes*
6 *stalks celery with leaves, chopped*
½ *cup chopped parsley*
2 *large onions, chopped*
2 *cloves garlic, minced*
1½ *tablespoons Worcestershire sauce*
2 *teaspoons soy sauce*
1½ *cups dry red wine*
1 *pound mushrooms, quartered*

Remove all excess fat from lamb shanks. Put flour, seasoned salt and pepper in paper bag and shake shanks in it to coat well. Put diced bacon in stewpot and render out fat, remove the bits of browned bacon and reserve. Brown shanks in hot bacon fat on all sides. Add bacon cracklings, tomatoes, celery, parsley,

38

onions, garlic, Worcestershire sauce, soy sauce and wine. Cover and simmer for about 2 hours. Add mushrooms and continue cooking for 25 minutes. *Serves 4.*

ALTHOUGH most stews cooked in the oven are called casseroles and therefore cannot legitimately be included in this cookbook, the following is so definitely a stew that it simply cannot be omitted. Anyhow, the recipe is one of those invented by my husband, who insists it's a stew, no matter what anyone else says. It can be cooked on top of the stove, too, in which case you don't seal the pot and cook it for just 1½ hours instead of the full 2 hours.

### OVEN-STEWED LAMB SHANKS

3 lamb shanks, cut in half
3 tablespoons flour
½ teaspoon seasoned salt
½ teaspoon freshly ground pepper
1 10½-ounce can chicken broth
½ cup sake
1 tablespoon soy sauce
1 cup flour
Sufficient water to make a paste

Remove all outer fat from the lamb shanks and put in stewpot over medium heat to render out the fat. Remove cracklings from pot and reserve. Put flour, seasoned salt and pepper in paper bag and shake the halved shanks in it to coat well. Pour off fat in excess of 3 tablespoons. Brown the floured shanks, taking care to start by setting shanks upright on cut ends and searing well to seal in juices. When shanks are well browned on all sides, remove and add seasoned flour to absorb any remaining fat. Add chicken broth, sake and soy sauce, blending well. Return shanks and cracklings to pot and cover. Make a stiff paste of flour and water and seal the lid to the pot. Place in a 350° oven for 2 hours. Crack the flour-and-water crust off the pot, and serve. The meat will be very tender and ready to drop from the bones. Egg noodles are a perfect accompaniment. *Serves 4 to 6.*


No COOKBOOK on stews would be complete without a recipe for mutton stew, although mutton is not nearly so easy to find these days as it once was. It is my impression that mutton is far more commonly used in Europe than it is in the United States, and the following recipe comes from Great Britain, where, presumably, they let their sheep get a little older before slaughtering them.

## MUTTON STEW

1 *carrot, sliced*
1 *medium onion, sliced*
4 *stalks celery, chopped*
4 *ounces olive oil*
½ *cup dry white wine*
2 *ounces wine vinegar*
1 *tablespoon chopped parsley*
¼ *teaspoon dried rosemary*
¼ *teaspoon thyme*
1 *bay leaf*
2 *cloves garlic*
5 *shallots*
1 *tablespoon peppercorns*
½ *teaspoon salt*
4 *pounds boned mutton, cubed*
¼ *pound bacon, diced*
5 *tablespoons olive oil*
4 *large onions, sliced*

Skin of ½ orange
2 tablespoons cognac
1 cup dried mushrooms (from a Chinese food
    store)
Boiling water to cover

Put the carrot, onion, celery and olive oil in a heavy
saucepan over medium heat and cook until lightly
browned. Add the wine and vinegar, parsley, rosemary,
thyme, bayleaf, garlic, shallots, peppercorns and salt.
Simmer for 30 minutes, then remove from fire and let
cool. Pour over the cubed mutton and let stand for at
least 6 hours. Strain the liquid and reserve, discarding
the herbs, garlic, shallots and peppercorns. Put the
bacon and olive oil in your stewpot and start cooking
over low heat. Add the onions and cook gently until
they are lightly browned. Add the mutton and the
strained marinade and orange skin. Turn heat to high
and let boil until reduced about a third. Add cognac
and mushrooms and enough boiling water to cover.
Cover the pot and reduce heat to very low simmer for
4 hours. After 3 hours, pour off liquid from top of stew
and place in freezing compartment to congeal excess
fat. At the end of the cooking time, lift off fat and discard, returning liquid to pot. *Serves 6 to 8.*


SOME of the fanciest and most complicated dishes in
the world are made with veal, probably because veal all
by its lonesome tends to be rather innocuous and because it lends itself to a great variety of treatments.
Unlike beef and lamb, veal must be watched very carefully while it is cooking, as it can easily be overcooked,
in which case it is dry and tasteless. There are few
things less interesting than a piece of veal that has been
allowed to lose all its juices. The rule for cooking veal
is to prick it with a fork now and then until the blood is
replaced by a colorless liquid; as soon as this happens,

zip it off the stove. You should be careful when reheating veal, too, for the same reason. With these cautions in mind, you can make some extremely flavorful stews with veal.

## BASIC VEAL STEW WITH VEGETABLES

2½ pounds boned leg of veal, in small cubes
6 tablespoons butter
4 medium onions, chopped
1 tablespoon paprika
2 medium tomatoes, quartered
1 green pepper, cored and sliced
¼ cup water
1 tablespoon capers
½ pint sour cream
Salt and pepper to taste

Have your butcher prepare the veal. Melt butter in stewpot over medium heat, and cook the onions until a very light golden brown. Add meat cubes and paprika, and continue cooking while the meat browns nicely, stirring often with a large spoon to brown evenly. Add tomatoes, green pepper and water. Cover and lower heat to a simmer for 45 minutes to 1 hour, adding a tablespoon or two of water if needed. Add capers and sour cream, and salt and pepper to taste. Turn off heat and allow to sit for 5 to 10 minutes before serving. *Serves 4 to 6.*

AT OUR HOUSE, veal in any form is a special-occasion dish, because it is neither plentiful nor inexpensive in Southern California. There are many cattle ranches hereabouts, but apparently all the calves are allowed to grow to maturity, as, according to our butcher, the only veal he gets (and that but once a week) is from Wisconsin! I like to pretend that it is a reasonable world and that there must be a reason for this, too, but so far it eludes me.

Anyhow, our veal recipes are all rather fancy, and require more time and attention than stews made with other meats. Still, the following sounds more complicated than it is, and the result is quite worth the trouble.

## VEAL STEW WITH TOMATOES AND ZUCCHINI

6 *good-size veal cutlets, about ¼ inch thick*
1 *heaping tablespoon flour*
½ *teaspoon salt*
¼ *teaspoon black pepper*
2 *tablespoons butter*
3 *tablespoons brandy*
1 *tablespoon butter*
1 *heaping teaspoon tomato paste*
3 *teaspoons instant flour*
1 *cup chicken broth*
½ *cup sake or dry white wine*
2 *scant teaspoons red currant jelly*
2 *medium zucchini, in thick slices*
1 *clove garlic, pressed*
4 *medium tomatoes, peeled and quartered*
½ *cup grated Parmesan cheese*
2 *tablespoons melted butter*

Pound each cutlet with your fist to flatten as much as possible. Mix flour, salt and pepper in paper bag and shake cutlets well to coat. Melt 2 tablespoons butter in stewpot until very hot (but not smoking) and place 2 or 3 cutlets in pot so they lie flat. Brown quickly on both sides. Repeat until all cutlets have been browned. Return all slices to pot and turn off fire. Pour brandy over them and ignite, stirring the meat and shaking pan as it flames. Remove meat from pot. With fire still off, add 1 tablespoon butter, tomato paste and instant flour, stirring well as you shake the flour in. Add the chicken broth, sake and currant jelly. Return to fire over medium heat, and add zucchini and garlic. Cover and boil gently for 5 minutes. Add tomatoes and put cutlets on top, cover and simmer 7 minutes, while your broiler is heating. Mix grated cheese with melted butter, sprinkle over top and slide under hot broiler for a few minutes until cheese browns. *Serves 6.*

To SERVE sour cream with veal seems one of the most natural things in the world; it is as harmonious a combination as pot roast and beer. The only drawback is one of color, and, as the following recipe uses small white onions, too, the result is one of white on white. I like to serve one of the pretty green vegetables (asparagus, say) with this dish, along with pickled beets or cranberry sauce to liven up the aesthetics of it.

## STEWED VEAL CHOPS WITH SOUR CREAM AND WINE

    4 tablespoons butter
    6 small white onions, sliced
    ½ pound fresh mushrooms, sliced
    1 large stalk celery with leaves, chopped
    1 tablespoon flour
    ½ teaspoon fines herbes (parsley, chives, chervil and
        thyme)
    1 cup beef bouillon
    1 cup sour cream
    ½ cup sake or dry white wine
    6 veal chops
    1 heaping tablespoon flour
    2 tablespoons butter
    3 tablespoons brandy

Melt 4 tablespoons butter in a heavy saucepan over

medium heat. Add onions, mushrooms and celery, and sauté until tender. Add flour and fines herbes and cook 3 minutes. Add bouillon, sour cream and sake. Turn heat to a very low simmer for 10 minutes, while you are preparing chops. Shake chops with 1 heaping tablespoon flour in a paper bag, and heat 2 tablespoons butter in your stewpot over high heat. Brown chops on both sides, turn off fire and pour brandy over them. Ignite and flame, shaking pot while brandy is burning. Pour your simmering sauce on top, cover and simmer over low heat for 30 minutes. *Serves 6.*

## VEAL STEW WITH ONIONS

2  *tablespoons flour*
½  *teaspoon salt*
½  *teaspoon freshly ground black pepper*
2½ *pounds boned veal shoulder, in small cubes*
2  *tablespoons butter*
1  *cup chicken broth*
½  *cup sake or dry white wine*
1  *teaspoon paprika*
1  *teaspoon grated nutmeg*
4  *onions, sliced*
1  *clove garlic, finely chopped*
1  *tablespoon chopped parsley*
1  *tablespoon sugar*
1  *cup sour cream*

Put flour, salt and pepper in a paper bag and shake cubes of veal in it to coat each piece well. Melt butter in stewpot over high heat and brown the cubes on all sides. Reduce heat to low and add chicken broth, sake, paprika and nutmeg. Throw in onions and garlic, parsley and sugar. Cover and simmer very, very slowly for 1½ to 2 hours, until meat is tender. Add sour cream and turn off heat for 10 minutes before serving. *Serves 4 to 6.*

If you have ever had osso buco, you will remember it as one of the best stews you ever tasted. It is made from veal knuckle, which is rich in gelatin, and is most marvelously delicious. Unfortunately, veal knuckle can be very hard to get (at least that has been my experience). If you have osso buco in mind, you would probably do well to remember your butcher's birthday and inquire about his children whenever you see him; perhaps, then, he will remember you when the next veal knuckle is available. No matter how much trouble it is to get, it is worth it.

## OSSO BUCO

5 tablespoons flour
1 teaspoon seasoned salt
1 veal knuckle, cut into 4 or 5 pieces
2 pounds veal (from around the knuckle), cubed
4 tablespoons bacon drippings
1½ cups chicken broth
½ cup sake or dry white wine
¾ cup tomato juice
½ cup water
¾ pound mushrooms, de-stemmed and whole

Put flour and seasoned salt in paper bag and shake the pieces of knuckle in bag. Heat bacon drippings in stewpot over moderately high heat and drop in the bones. Let brown on both sides and remove. Shake cubed veal in the seasoned flour, and brown the pieces on all sides. Remove meat from pot and absorb all remaining fat with flour. Return bones to pot and place browned pieces of veal on top of them. Add chicken broth, sake, tomato juice and water, cover tightly and simmer very gently for 2 hours. Add mushrooms and continue cooking for another half hour. *Serves 6 to 8.*

VEAL is so splendidly versatile that you can combine it with almost anything and be fairly certain of a good result. While collecting material for this book, it was hard to know where to stop when I came to veal, but stop I did, with the following two excellent stews which will make your reputation as a cook.

## VEAL STEWED IN BEER

*2  tablespoons flour*
*2½  pounds boned veal shoulder, in 1-inch cubes*
*2  tablespoons butter*
*2  12-ounce cans beer*
*2  medium onions, sliced*
*2  tomatoes, peeled and quartered*
*2  bay leaves*
*8  whole cloves*
*½  teaspoon fines herbes (parsley, chives, chervil and thyme)*
*¼  teaspoon Tabasco sauce*
*Salt and pepper to taste*
*1  tablespoon lemon juice*

Put flour in paper bag and shake veal cubes well to coat. Melt butter in stewpot over high heat and brown cubes lightly. Reduce heat and add beer, onions, tomatoes, bay leaves, cloves, fines herbes, Tabasco sauce. Season with salt and pepper to taste (not much will be needed). Cover and simmer very, very slowly for 1½ to 2 hours, until meat is just nicely tender. Add lemon juice at the end, and serve. *Serves 4 to 6.*

## VEAL STEWED IN RED WINE

*2  tablespoons butter*
*2  pounds boned veal shoulder, in 1-inch cubes*

47

3  tablespoons flour
More butter if needed
2  cups beef bouillon
1  cup good dry red wine
½  teaspoon salt
8  peppercorns
1  teaspoon paprika
1  tablespoon chopped parsley
1  bay leaf
¼  teaspoon thyme
8  small whole white onions
½  pound button mushrooms

Melt butter in stewpot and brown veal cubes on all
sides. Add flour and more butter if needed to take up
the flour. Reduce heat to very low and add all other ingredients. Simmer very, very slowly for 1½ hours, or
until meat is just tender. *Serves 4.*

IN ALL my researching for this book, I have not encountered a single recipe for a stew made with pork in
the traditional way, i.e., meat cut in cubes and stewed
in gravy with vegetables. I don't know why this is, particularly in view of the fact that pork chops are wonderful when stewed. The meat is never dry and stringy,
as it can easily be when the chops are broiled or sautéed, and the gravy is wonderful on potatoes or rice.
The following recipe is regularly served at our house
accompanied by okra and yams.

## PORK CHOPS STEWED IN MILK

4  loin pork chops, ¾ inch thick
2  tablespoons flour
½  teaspoon seasoned salt
¼  teaspoon freshly ground pepper
1  to 2 cups milk

Remove all excess fat from chops and drop it into stewpot over medium heat. Render out the cracklings, remove from pot and reserve. Put flour, salt and pepper in paper bag, and shake chops well to coat. Brown chops on both sides in hot fat, and if there is excess fat in pot, add enough of the flour from the bag to absorb it. Turn heat to very low, and add milk enough to form a medium-thick gravy. Cover and simmer for 1 hour, checking occasionally and adding milk if needed to prevent the gravy from becoming too thick. *Serves 4.*

THE FIRST TIME I encountered the following recipe, I thought it was ridiculous and said so. But my husband was either more perspicacious or more adventurous than I and decided to try it. It was—and is—a great success; the peanut butter and the onion and the mushroom soup all blend together, so that they lose their individual identities and achieve a brand-new one that is exceedingly pleasant to the palate. Try it, and you will agree.

## PORK CHOPS STEWED WITH ONION AND PEANUT BUTTER

*4  loin pork chops, ¾ inch thick*
*2  tablespoons flour*
*½  teaspoon seasoned salt*
*¼  teaspoon freshly ground pepper*
*4  thick slices onion*
*1  10½-ounce can cream of mushroom soup*
*1  cup peanut butter*
*1  tablespoon Worcestershire sauce*
*2  tablespoons sake or dry white wine*
*1  to 2 cups milk, as needed*

Remove all excess fat from chops and drop the pieces

into your stewpot over medium heat. Render out the cracklings, remove from pot and reserve. Put flour, salt and pepper in paper bag, and shake chops in it well. Brown chops on both sides, and if excess fat remains in pot, add seasoned flour to absorb it. Reduce heat to very low, and put a thick slice of onion on top of each chop. Mix together the mushroom soup, peanut butter, Worcestershire sauce and sake. Add a cup of milk to start, and pour this mixture over the slices of onion and pork chops. Cover and simmer very slowly for at least 1 hour, until onion slices are tender. Lift chops from bottom occasionally to be certain they don't stick, and add milk if needed to keep the gravy thick, but not too thick. *Serves 4.*

MY HUSBAND and I are inclined to feel that a stew profits from the addition of wine, even if only half a cup (sometimes more than this amount would be ruinous), or brandy, even if only a tablespoonful. If you don't care for either of these liquors, try sprinkling a little Calvados in your stew; it will provide a very nice lilt.

Wine is definitely requested in the following recipe. If you resist the idea of wine in cooking, or really and truly don't like the taste, you can substitute chicken broth or a very mild beef bouillon. In that event, you may find it necessary to use a little more seasoning.

## PORK CHOPS STEWED IN WINE

6 *pork chops, at least 1 inch thick*
1 *heaping tablespoon flour*
1 *cup consommé*
½ *cup sake or dry white wine*
*Salt and pepper to taste*
2 *tablespoons sweet pickle relish*
1 *teaspoon Dijon mustard*

Remove excess fat from pork chops and drop it into stewpot over hot fire. Render out the cracklings. Remove cracklings and reserve. Brown pork chops in hot fat on both sides. Pour off most of the fat (if there is any excess) and stir in flour. Add consommé and sake, reduce heat to very low and season with salt and pepper to taste. Simmer for 30 minutes, or until chops are tender. Add relish and mustard and turn off fire for 10 minutes before serving. *Serves 6.*

I HAD to stretch my definition of a stew in order to include the following recipe, with which this chapter is concluded, but I could no more resist writing about these meatballs than you will be able to resist eating them. The recipe is the result of much experimentation, with my husband and me each contributing a soupçon of this and a dash of that to bring the meatballs to the point of perfection. Because of the work that went into them, they have been honored with the name we have given to our home, which, in turn, comes from my husband's fictional detective character, Michael Shayne.

You can, of course, serve the meatballs without the sauce, and if you roll them no larger than pecans, they make marvelous hors d'oeuvres. They are delicious, distinctive and daring, but a word of warning is required: Don't cheat on this recipe, or you'll end up with plain, ordinary meatballs that anyone might make.

## STEWED MEATBALLS, SHANTY SHAYNE

*4 slices white bread*
*¼ cup beef bouillon*
*¼ cup water*
*1 pound ground beef (neck, shoulder or chuck)*
*1 medium onion, quartered*
*1 large clove garlic, pressed*

1 teaspoon chili powder
½ teaspoon curry powder
1 teaspoon seasoned salt
¼ teaspoon Tabasco sauce
Butter, as needed
Brandy or rum, as needed

Soak the bread in bouillon and water in a large bowl. Knead the meat into the bread with your fingers to mix thoroughly. Nothing will substitute for fingers for this job. Put the quartered onion into the blender with just a little bouillon to moisten, and blend thoroughly. Add blended onion, garlic, chili powder, curry powder, seasoned salt and Tabasco sauce to the meat and bread mixture, and again knead well with your fingers. Roll into balls between your palms, handling very gently. *This recipe will make between 25 and 50 balls, depending on size.*

Put two heavy frying pans over moderate heat and melt a little butter in each. Place the meatballs in the butter carefully, without crowding, and brown on all sides, turning with a spoon and taking care to keep them in one piece, because they are easily broken. When each panful is browned, pour in a generous ¼ cup of warmed light rum or brandy (whichever you prefer) and ignite. Flame each pan of cooked meatballs by shaking pan vigorously until flame goes out. Remove meatballs to your stewpot, pouring the liquid over each batch and wiping the pan with a paper towel, adding butter for the next batch. When all are cooked and in your pot, set it over the very lowest flame possible and let them stew in their own delectable juices for 1 hour (or until you are ready to serve). These are also wonderful to go into a tomato sauce for spaghetti or simply served as a main course. *Serves from 6 to 12.*

# 2

## CHICKENS, YOUNG AND OLD

*(Poultry Stews)*

WHEN I was a little girl, my mother always kept chickens. In March or early April, she would come home with a boxful of tiny, peep-peeping morsels of yellow fluff, which would be kept in a warm corner of the kitchen until the weather was clement enough and the baby chicks tough enough to be transferred outdoors. There ensued a period of suspense during which the chickens identified themselves as "layers" and "non-layers," and, although Mother was very fond of her chickens, she was absolutely ruthless, an unproductive hen being given very little time to laze around the yard before winding up in the frying pan or the stewpot. The chickens must have understood this, for, throughout my childhood, chicken was a special, company dish. From this, I must conclude that most of Mother's chickens laid eggs furiously until well into the fall, when they were sold and ended up in somebody else's roasting pan or stewpot.

Today, my husband and I find it worth the time and effort to drive eight miles to a poultry market that deals exclusively in the finest unfrozen poultry, and is staffed by experts eager to skillfully dissect their product exactly according to our specifications. And today I would guess that chicken is served at our house two or even three times as often as it appeared on my mother's table. Probably the most telling reason for this is that it is a whole lot easier to drive eight miles to a poultry market and come home with a "nice, plump stewing hen," all clean and neat and ready for the pot, than it was to walk out into the yard and catch a chicken, then kill it, pull off the feathers, singe the pin feathers and remove and dispose of the entrails before you were even ready to consider what size pot would hold it.

Apart from the messiness of personal slaughter, there are other reasons for the popularity of chicken at our house. For one thing, it is certainly the most economical form of meat available today. In another chapter of this book called "Saving Pennies (Economy Stews)," there is a recipe for a stew that will adequately serve 6, made with chicken backs and wings which costs, altogether, $1.06. I'm not positive but I think that includes the cost of the gas for cooking. While the cost of other meat, most notably beef, goes skyrocketing along in never-never land, chicken continues to be available at a price that's close to reasonable.

Most important of all, perhaps, chicken is extraordinarily versatile. At our market, it is available in truly astonishing variety, classified according to age, size and method of cooking, or cut up into pieces so that you need buy only those portions which tempt you. Consider the fact that chicken livers—surely as luxurious an item as hummingbirds' tongues—can be bought by the pound, and drumsticks—of which there were never more than two at a time when I was a child—are available by the dozen. About the only parts of the chicken which we have been unable to obtain at our market are the feet, for some unknown reason. Feet are marvelous flavoring agents for soups (and therefore for the broth that goes into stews), and if you can get them, by all means do so.

A bit of advice about buying chicken in parts is to watch out that you get only what you think you are paying for. Most supermarkets cut up their chickens in such a way that the higher priced portions include meat and bone which, when sold separately, are far less costly. The thigh, for example, often has part of the back still attached to it—which is a little bit like the good old days when some butchers charged for the weight of their thumbs. A reputable poultry dealer does not engage in such practices, and he is also a dependable source of supply for an honestly "fresh" holiday turkey as well as the succulent thing of beauty that is the subject of this chapter: the stewing hen.

The versatility of chicken is compounded by the fact that it can be cooked in so many different ways and lends itself to so many plain and fancy sauces. You can bake, broil, fry, fricassee, roast, toast and barbecue your chicken, and eat it plain or serve it in or with a sauce made with wine (any color), cream (sweet or sour), fruit juice or that item without which no self-respecting kitchen can function: chicken broth. You can season it with almost any of the herbs, beginning, of course, with sage; you can curry it, mold it in gelatin, grind it into croquettes or quenelles, stuff it with anything from bread crumbs to potatoes and chestnuts, slice it into sandwiches or even lose it in a salad.

On the other hand—you can stew it!

A chicken stew does not necessarily require a stewing chicken. In some cases it is advisable, in fact, to use younger birds, as they cook more quickly and make prettier servings. Historically, a proper stewing hen is an old, tired biddy, well past her prime, with stringy thighs, sunken breasts and scarcely a morsel of fat to be found on her body. Fortunately, it is almost impossible to buy that kind of a chicken today. I think they must all be consigned to those commercial establishments that produce such unappetizing items as canned chicken, bouillon cubes and frozen TV dinners.

Today's stewing chicken obviously spent her declining days doing nothing but sitting around and getting fat. She's a plump thing, weighing between five and eight pounds, with heavy breasts and thighs and great pockets of rich, yellowish fat. People are so afraid of fat these days that many of them trim this fat away, all the while muttering curses under their breaths, and toss it into whatever they use as a garbage disposal. Anyone who commits such a criminal act ought never to be allowed to enter another kitchen. Leave the fat in place and you will have a very rich and flavorsome broth from which the excess fat may be skimmed and reserved for later use such as sautéing chicken livers or any other product that might benefit from the flavor of chicken fat.

A stewing chicken must be simmered very slowly for a long time before the meat is tender enough to eat; in fact, the meat should literally fall off the bone. This makes it an ideal fowl to use in those dishes that require cooked, boned chicken, as it is economical and does not need a person with a medical degree to perform the boning. A stewing chicken is also what you want for any of those delectable dishes involving dumplings, because a dumpling must be dressed in lots and lots of broth.

And a stewing chicken is absolutely necessary for making chicken broth, which is where this chapter properly begins.

YOU MAY QUIBBLE and contend that chicken broth is a soup rather than a stew, and you would be right, but there could scarcely be a chapter on chicken stews at all unless it began with broth. Chicken stews *begin* with chicken broth, and homemade chicken broth is far superior to any prepared product. (Remember how the goodwives in the old books were always running over to the sick neighbor's with a jar of freshly made chicken broth? Now the neighbor goes to the doctor and gets a shot of penicillin and we lose another opportunity to prove ourselves good neighbors.) I confess that I don't always have a homemade broth on hand in my house (although I try to), but I do keep a goodly supply of the better substitutes in the cupboard at all times. Powdered chicken broth is the best, as you can have it as strong as you like. Next come the canned chicken broths, of which the concentrated form is preferable, as it is easier to dilute a broth than to try to make it stronger. However, chicken bouillon cubes are eschewed, as they are altogether too insipid. Drink them if you like, but don't use them in your cooking.

## CHICKEN BROTH

*1 stewing hen, 5 to 6 pounds, cut in pieces*
*Cold water to cover*
*1 bay leaf*
*8 to 10 peppercorns*
*1 carrot*
*1 onion, quartered*
*1 clove garlic, halved*
*1 stalk celery with leaves, cut in several pieces*

Put all ingredients in a big, heavy stewpot. Bring to a brisk boil for about 5 minutes. Turn off heat and skim any scum off the top. Turn fire to a very slow simmer and cook, covered, for 6 hours, adding hot water as needed. Strain off the broth for future reference, throw away the vegetables, and use the chicken for something else (see below). *Yields about 1 quart of broth.*

Note that this recipe does not include any salt or other strong seasoning. This is because it is basically a stock rather than a soup, and you want to keep it flexible. You can boil it down to strengthen the flavor or to make chicken jelly. Or you can season it with anything in the wide-wide world that will be agreeable to the dish in which you are incorporating it. The chicken meat that you take out will be somewhat lacking in flavor, but you can always figure a way around that. Grind it up and make croquettes out of it; my husband does this and it is a real gourmet treat. Or you can chop it, season it, mix in some pickle relish and use it in sandwiches.

Now that you have a quart or two of chicken broth in your refrigerator, you can go on to some of the marvelous things you can do with it. In my opinion, just about the most marvelous of these is chicken and dumplings. My memories of childhood contain many references to this dish, but it seems to me there was never enough sauce for the dumplings—the last dumpling on the platter always sat there looking woefully dry and friendless. When I started being serious about cooking, I resolved that this would never happen at my table, so the following recipe provides plenty of sauce for all the dumplings you can squeeze in on top of the pot. This is not as simple as it sounds, for the broth thickens considerably after the dumplings are added and as they cook.

## CHICKEN AND DUMPLINGS

*1  stewing hen, 5 to 6 pounds*
*3  tablespoons flour*
*1  large onion, finely sliced*
*Chicken broth and water in equal quantities*
*1  stalk celery, finely sliced*
*Salt to taste*

**DUMPLINGS**

*1½  cups flour (or more, if you have a large pot)*
*½  teaspoon salt*
*3  heaping teaspoons double-acting baking powder
   (or more, as with the flour)*
*⅔  cup milk (or more)*

Disjoint the hen and tear out extra rolls of fat at rear end. Cut the fat into small pieces and fry out in the bottom of the largest stewpot you have. Put flour in paper bag and shake chicken pieces to coat well. When fat has been reduced to cracklings, remove them and drop pieces of chicken into hot fat and brown nicely on all sides, removing browned pieces and adding others until all are browned. Remove the last pieces and add onion. Sauté until golden brown. Return browned chicken to pot and add half broth and half water to cover well. Add celery, and salt to taste. Bring to a slow simmer and cook, covered, for 2 hours, or until chicken is nicely tender but not ready to fall from bones. Make dumplings by sifting together flour, salt and baking powder in a large mixing bowl. If you are lucky enough to have a pot larger than 9 inches, increase quantities of flour, baking powder and milk to fit the larger pot. (You will have to guess at this the first time, but the idea is to get as many dumplings in as will fit comfortably.) Add milk gradually to mixing bowl, stirring as you go to produce a dough which should be as dry as possible and still moist enough to spoon up, but must be pushed off the spoon with your finger. Drop heaping teaspoons of the dough into pot after bringing it to a rolling boil. Don't overcrowd even if you have a little dough left over. Cover tightly and boil for 18 minutes. Lift dumplings out separately into large serving dish, arrange chicken on platter and pour sauce over both chicken and dumplings. *Serves 6 to 8.*


AT THIS POINT, there may be a hue and cry about what constitutes a dumpling. A friend of ours who hails from Alabama insists that a dumpling must be made from rolled-out dough cut into strips. We say that this is a noodle, but she does not agree, pointing out that a proper noodle is dried before use. And so the argument goes. The following recipe is included in this cookbook with a special dedication to Lucy.

## CHICKEN AND (NOODLES) DUMPLINGS

*1 stewing hen, 5 to 6 pounds*

DUMPLINGS

*1½ cups flour*
*½ teaspoon salt*
*1 egg*
*3 to 4 tablespoons milk*
*3 tablespoons butter*

Cook chicken as in Chicken and Dumplings recipe. Make dumplings after 1½ hours as follows: Sift flour and salt into mixing bowl, stir in the egg and add milk to make a very thick dough, adding milk sparingly after 3 tablespoons. Roll out on lightly floured board to about ⅛ inch thickness, and cut into 2-inch squares. When chicken is tender but not dropping from bone, remove chicken and raise heat to a rolling boil and drop the squares in. Boil 20 minutes. Remove dumplings to a colander and drain well, and drench with butter before putting in serving dish. *Serves 6.*

THERE ARE many other types of dumplings which could be discussed endlessly; in fact, I could parley chicken and dumplings into a major portion of this chapter, making the dumplings out of raw potatoes or cooked potatoes or corn meal. Some restraint is in order, however, and the subject of dumplings will be closed with one more recipe, using one of the delights of Jewish cuisine, the matzo-ball dumpling. A word of warning here: If these dumplings do not come out of the pot as light and tender as a butterfly's kiss, throw them away

60

and try again. Incorrectly made, matzo-ball dumplings are as hard and tough as golf balls and about as easy to digest.

## CHICKEN WITH MATZO BALLS

*1 stewing hen, 5 to 6 pounds*

DUMPLINGS

*1 cup matzo meal*
*1 cup boiling water*
*3 tablespoons melted chicken fat*
*2 eggs, separated*
*1 teaspoon salt*
*¼ teaspoon white pepper*
*1 tablespoon finely chopped parsley*

Prepare the stewing hen as in Chicken and Dumplings recipe, and simmer 2 hours. Make the matzo-ball dumplings at least 1 hour before cooking, as follows: Mix matzo meal and boiling water in a bowl, add chicken fat and egg yolks, beating well. Add salt, pepper and parsley, and fold in egg whites, beaten until stiff but not dry. Chill, covered, for 1 hour. Dip your hands in cold water and roll into 1-inch balls between wet palms. Raise the heat slightly and drop the balls into the broth in which the chicken was cooked. Cook, covered, for 15 minutes. *Serves 6.*

MANY COOKS make a definite distinction between stewed chicken and fricasseed chicken, holding that stewed chicken should not be browned before liquid is added. My husband and I feel that the flavor is definitely improved by browning, so the preceding three recipes might be called "fricastews," I guess. However, there is a minor distinction in my mind. Stewed chicken is cooked in clear liquid, while a fricassee is stewed in a sauce. With that technicality out of the way, here is:

## BASIC CHICKEN FRICASSEE

1 *young roasting hen, 4 to 5 pounds*
3 *tablespoons flour*
1 *teaspoon seasoned salt*
½ *teaspoon pepper*
3 *tablespoons butter*
3 *cups chicken broth (more if needed)*
*Salt to taste*
1 *tablespoon instant flour (or more)*
1 *heaping teaspoon fines herbes (parsley, chives, chervil and thyme)*
8 *small white onions*
½ *pound small white mushrooms, sliced*

Remove lumps of fat from rear of chicken. Put flour, seasoned salt and pepper in a paper bag and shake chicken pieces in it to coat well. Put butter in the stewpot and heat well, then brown chicken pieces carefully (adding more butter if needed) over moderate heat. Pour in the broth, add salt to taste. Remove from fire and add just enough instant flour to form a very light sauce. Return to fire and bring to a gentle simmer. Add fines herbes, cover and simmer gently for 1½ hours, or until chicken is nicely tender but not ready to fall from bones. Add onions and mushrooms (and more broth if sauce is too thick) and continue cooking about 15 minutes, until vegetables are tender. *Serves 4.*

OBVIOUSLY, the fricassee is capable of infinite variation, and you probably have a favorite combination of your own except that you might not have realized that's what it was. Following is a fricassee, Creole-style, and you can omit the shrimp, although that would be rather a pity.

## CHICKEN AND SHRIMP FRICASSEE

6 *frying chicken legs (or breasts, as you prefer)*
3 *tablespoons flour*
3 *tablespoons butter (or more)*
2 *medium onions, thinly sliced*
1 *large can Italian tomatoes*
1 *large clove garlic, pressed*
1 *bay leaf, crushed*
½ *teaspoon fines herbes (parsley, chives, chervil and*
    *thyme)*
¼ *teaspoon Tabasco sauce*
*Salt and pepper to taste*
1½ *pounds shelled and deveined raw shrimp*

Shake chicken legs with flour in a paper bag, and sauté in butter in the bottom of stewpot until very lightly browned. Remove chicken and set aside. Sauté sliced onion in remaining butter (adding more if needed), then add tomatoes, garlic and seasonings, and simmer, uncovered, 25 minutes. Return chicken to the sauce and continue to simmer for 20 minutes. Add shrimp and cook another 15 minutes. *Serves 6.*

I SUPPOSE that, technically, this one is also a fricassee, although I find that I balk at describing anything cooked in wine and brandy and cream as "just" a fricassee. This makes a wonderful party dish if you can find a nice plump frying chicken. If you use a roaster, it will require a little more cooking time, and you must watch the liquid carefully, adding more wine or water if needed.

# CHICKEN IN BRANDY AND CREAM

*1 frying chicken, 3 to 4 pounds*
*3 tablespoons butter*
*2 cloves garlic, halved*
*1 cup white wine*
*¼ cup your best brandy*
*1 cup heavy cream*
*2 egg yolks*

Have the chicken disjointed. Put butter in stewpot on fairly high heat, and drop chicken and garlic into it, turning chicken frequently to brown well on all sides. Remove the pieces of garlic, add wine and brandy and bring to a boil. As soon as it boils, touch a match to it and shake pan vigorously until flame goes out. Cover and simmer for 20 minutes (longer for a roasting chicken). Remove tender chicken to warm oven. Add cream and egg yolks to sauce in stewpot and simmer until thickened. Pour over warm chicken pieces. *Serves 4.*

WHEN I started collecting material for this book, I invited a group of ladies for lunch, making sure that my guest list included all the best cooks in town, as I planned to pick their brains for stew recipes. One of my guests said that she thought a stew cookbook was a marvelous idea, but she hoped I would not include a recipe for Brunswick stew because every cookbook on her shelf had one and she was tired of reading about it. I promised her I would omit Brunswick stew from my next cookbook, but that this one would have to include it in order to remain respectable. It's a healthy, hearty dish, and one may tire of reading about it, but never of eating it.

# BRUNSWICK STEW

1 roasting hen, 5 to 6 pounds, disjointed
3 tablespoons bacon drippings
1 medium onion, sliced
1½ cups tomatoes, peeled, quartered and seeded
1½ pounds fresh lima beans, or 2 packages frozen
1 cup chicken broth
3 whole cloves
Salt and pepper to taste
3 cups corn, cut from cob or frozen
2 teaspoons Worcestershire sauce
1 cup toasted bread crumbs

Brown the pieces of chicken in bacon drippings in your stewpot. Remove the last pieces of chicken and sauté the onion until golden brown. Return chicken to pot, add tomatoes, lima beans, chicken broth and cloves. Salt and pepper to taste. Cover and simmer for 1½ hours, or until chicken is nicely tender. Add corn and continue cooking until meat is ready to drop from bones. Add Worcestershire sauce and stir in bread crumbs. Serve at once. *Serves 8.*

NORMALLY, one definitely associates oranges with ducks. Probably because they do make such a palatable combination, the orange has come to be regarded as virtually the exclusive property of the duck, as far as poultry cookery is concerned. Not so, as you will discover if you have the courage to try the following recipe. And don't skip the Cointreau!

## CHICKEN STEWED IN ORANGE SAUCE

3 tablespoons flour
½ teaspoon salt
1 large broiler, disjointed

5 tablespoons butter
¼ teaspoon cinnamon
Dash ground cloves
1½ cups orange juice
¼ teaspoon Tabasco sauce
⅓ cup Cointreau
½ cup finely chopped almonds
½ cup raisins
1 orange, peeled, sectioned and deseeded

Put flour and salt in paper bag and shake chicken pieces in it to coat well. Melt butter in stewpot and brown chicken to golden. Remove from pot, and if you have butter remaining, add salted flour from the bag to absorb it all. Add spices and stir into a smooth paste. Add orange juice and Tabasco sauce slowly, stirring until it comes to a boil. (If too thick, thin with chicken broth to thin consistency.) Add browned chicken, Cointreau, almonds and raisins. Cover and simmer gently 45 minutes. Add sections of orange and cook 5 minutes. Remove chicken to warm platter and pour some of the sauce over it. The remaining sauce is wonderfully good on top of well-drained wild rice. *Serves 4.*

CHICKEN MARENGO was invented by Napoleon's chef one evening when he found himself near the village of Marengo in northern Italy, with dinnertime approaching far more rapidly than his supply train. The story goes that the worried but obviously quite resourceful chef concocted a meal for his irascible and hungry boss out of whatever he could scrounge from the countryside, including a squawking old hen. But what, precisely, those ingredients were (aside from the hen) remains a mystery, because chefs in those days—even famous ones—did not write things down. (Professional jealousy, I suspect.) Anyhow, if you have nothing better to do some rainy afternoon, you might go through a collection of cookbooks and consider the wide variety of recipes that are presented as chicken Marengo. About the only ingredient consistently included is tomato, although the more sophisticated cooks also agree on white wine and garlic, on the theory, I suppose, that no respectable French chef would think of cooking a chicken in water—particularly Italian water. Some recipes call for olive oil, some for butter; some use onions, others olives, and at least one resolved the controversy by using both. The majority opinion is that the chicken was stewed on top of the stove (which is the reason it is in this cookbook), but I have seen versions that called for baking in the oven.

Whatever it was that came into the chef's hands and stewpot that day in 1800 when Napoleon defeated the Austrians, this is the version that is served at our house, and we think you will agree that it is a masterpiece.

## CHICKEN MARENGO

*3 tablespoons flour*
*1 teaspoon seasoned salt*
*½ teaspoon freshly ground pepper*
*2 good-size broilers, disjointed*
*⅓ cup olive oil*
*2 medium onions, sliced*
*1 large clove garlic, pressed*
*½ pound mushrooms, sliced*
*1 large can Italian tomatoes*
*1 cup dry white wine*
*½ cup chicken broth*
*¼ cup good brandy*
*1 tablespoon tomato paste*
*Salt and pepper to taste*
*Instant flour*

Put flour, seasoned salt and pepper in paper bag and shake chicken pieces in it. Heat olive oil in your stewpot and brown chicken on all sides to golden. Remove from pot, then put in the sliced onions, garlic and mushrooms. Cook slowly, stirring frequently and adding more oil if needed, until mushrooms are tender. Add tomatoes, wine, chicken broth, brandy and tomato paste. Salt and pepper to taste. While hot but before it reaches a boil, stir in enough instant flour to form a very thin sauce. Cover and simmer gently 10 minutes. Add the browned chicken and simmer, covered, 45 minutes, or until chicken is thoroughly tender. *Serves 6.*

CREOLE COOKERY is something unique to this country and derives from the gradual melding of French and Spanish cooking that took place down Louisiana way. I don't know quite what it is that makes a dish Creole— the dictionary says things about peppers and tomatoes and seasonings, but it's mostly a matter of your point of view. Creole cooking has a piquancy, a daring, that is not present in purely French or Spanish cooking, so if your seasoning fingers are feeling generous, try this dish.

## CHICKEN CREOLE

6  *tablespoons butter*
2  *broilers, 2 pounds, quartered*
3  *tablespoons flour*
1  *teaspoon seasoned salt*
½  *teaspoon seasoned pepper*
1  *large onion, chopped*
2  *green peppers, seeded and quartered*
2  *tomatoes, seeded and quartered*
8  *stuffed green olives*
½  *pound fresh mushrooms, sliced*
1  *small can pimientos, cut in small pieces*

1 tablespoon chopped parsley
½ teaspoon fines herbes (chives, chervil and thyme)
Salt and pepper to taste
½ cup dry white wine
½ cup chicken broth
¼ cup good brandy

Melt butter in stewpot. Shake chicken quarters with flour and seasoned salt and pepper in a paper bag, and brown nicely in hot butter. Remove chicken. Add onion and green peppers, and shake in just enough seasoned flour from the bag to absorb the remaining butter in pot. Cook at low heat, stirring frequently, until flour is lightly browned. Add tomatoes, olives, mushrooms, pimientos, parsley and seasonings, and simmer 10 minutes. Return chicken to pot, add wine and broth and bring to boil. Reduce heat to simmer and cook for 45 minutes. Stir in brandy and serve at once. *Serves 4.*

You PROBABLY have as many recipes for chicken paprika as you have Hungarian friends (we happen to have several), but I have noticed that, although Hungarians are frequently excellent cooks, they are constitutionally unable to tell you how they do it. I suspect that they grind their own paprika secretly, reciting special charms as they do so, for if you complain that your chicken paprika did not turn out as well as theirs, they will exclaim, "Well, my dear, what did you expect, using *that* kind of paprika?" The following recipe uses the kind of paprika you can buy in a supermarket and tastes extremely fine. By the way, you can substitute sour cream for the sweet cream to achieve a slightly different, but no less delicious, flavor.

# CHICKEN PAPRIKA

*6 tablespoons sweet butter*
*2 good-size broilers, disjointed*
*3 medium onions, chopped*
*1 tablespoon paprika (or more)*
*½ cup chicken broth*
*Salt and pepper to taste*
*½ pint sweet cream (or sour)*

Melt butter in stewpot and brown all pieces of chicken evenly, adding onions to the last batch when there is room. Add paprika to give the chicken a nice reddish color. Add chicken broth, and salt and pepper to taste. Cover and stew 45 minutes. When chicken is tender, remove from pot and add cream to sauce. Cook just a few minutes to blend, and pour over chicken pieces. *Serves 6.*

AND, finally, here is a recipe for a chicken stew with vegetables which developed the way all good stews develop—with a pinch of this, a little of that, a drop of this, a soupçon of that. Created by Napoleon's chef, it would have been given a fancy name and discussed in history texts as well as cookbooks. As it is, it is the sort of stew that is developed in nearly every kitchen in the country. It is eaten in quantity, praised seldom and quickly forgotten, but it is just as much a triumph of culinary skill as any of those stews with more elegant names. Here is the version that is the favorite at my house:

## CHICKEN STEW, SHANTY SHAYNE

*1 stewing hen, 5 to 6 pounds, disjointed*
*3 tablespoons flour*
*Butter (if needed)*

70

2  onions, finely sliced
4  cups water
1  package chicken noodle soup mix
Salt  to  taste
2  dry bay leaves, crushed
8  peppercorns
6  cloves
½  cup fresh celery leaves
½  cup sake or dry white wine
1  tablespoon Worcestershire sauce
1  cup fresh peas, or 1 package frozen
4  carrots, sliced in rounds
12 to 16 pearl onions
3  medium potatoes (or yams), quartered

Remove rolls of fat from rear of chicken. Cut into small pieces and reduce to cracklings in your stewpot. Put flour in a paper bag and shake chicken pieces to coat. Remove cracklings from pot and brown chicken on all sides, adding more butter if needed. Add onions and water, bring to a fast boil and drop in dry soup mix. Add salt to taste. Cover and reduce heat to slow simmer. Make a bouquet garni by putting bay leaves, peppercorns, cloves and celery leaves in a small cheesecloth bag and add to pot. Simmer 1½ hours, or until chicken thighs will take a fork but are not fully done. Add sake, Worcestershire sauce, peas, carrots and pearl onions, and simmer 6 minutes. Drop in potatoes and cook until tender, about 15 minutes. *Serves 8.*

# 3

## UNDERWATER DENIZENS

### (Fish Stews)

As is the case with any strict rule governing public behavior or private morality, the directive that a stew must be simmered for a long, long time has its exception. And the exception must be honored as carefully as the rule. It concerns fish.

The fish does not profit by lengthy simmering, or by any other lengthy form of cooking. The longer you cook a fish, the stubborner, drier and less flavorsome it becomes. It is rather like the egg in the matter of cooking, and the wise cook would do well to remember the egg when she sets out to cook a piece of fish.

The disastrous results of overcooking fish are most clearly demonstrated by the noble abalone, California's home-grown delicacy which is easily on a par with Eastern bay scallops or fresh shad. Abalone belongs to the muscular fish family whose more familiar members include shrimp and clams, and if abalone is cooked for more than five minutes, it might as well be reserved for patching the tires on your automobile, as it becomes literally inedible and there is no way to undo the damage except with the meat grinder. Or better still, the cat.

The nonmuscular fish, like sole and halibut, doesn't get tough; it dries out or flakes apart. Some of the stews in this chapter call for fairly lengthy cooking times, and in such cases the fish must be handled very carefully to keep it in large pieces.

The fact that the fish itself is not going to be stewed indefinitely does not, however, eliminate it as a stew in~edient. Some of the most elegant dishes in the world are made with fish and are basically stews, no matter what the pseudonyms under which they appear. One of these stews with a loaf of French or Italian bread and a bottle of wine is sheer poetry. Try it some evening when you feel the need for something magical, something irresistible, something approaching perfection. And if you prefer red wine to white, thumb your nose at the connoisseurs and serve it.

My husband and I are fortunate in that we live near the Pacific Ocean and are able to get some variety of fresh fish the year around. If you live in the middle of the country and have any fishermen (or women) in the family, you can have truly fresh, fresh-water fish, than which there are few things more scrumptious. Today's quick-freezing methods make the denizens of the deep available to nearly everybody, but it is sad to have to observe that the quality of frozen fish is undependable, due to sloppy handling procedures from the processor's deep-freeze units to your grocer's freezer cabinets. And it is just not possible to determine by looking at the package whether or not it was permitted to thaw, partially or completely, at some point along its distribution journey. If you must use frozen fish, I can only wish you luck.

As for canned fish, it simply does not enter into the discussion. There is as little similarity between canned fish and fresh or frozen fish as there is between a tomato and a tamale. Perhaps exceptions could be made for canned crab meat, clams or Willapoint oysters, but, by and large, do not attempt to substitute canned fish in any of the recipes in this chapter unless it is specifically indicated that it is possible.

Another note: Most fish (as opposed to shellfish)

stews do not take kindly to reheating, as the fish tends to break up and get mushy.

BASIC to making stews with fish is the court bouillon, which is a fancy name for fish broth. Actually, the term applies to any seasoned liquid which has been cooked for a short time, but you will bump into it most frequently in connection with fish. Court bouillon is not available in cubes, powders or cans, but must be concocted, every time you need it, by your own delicate hands in your own kitchen. Do not be alarmed, however; most of the recipes in this chapter include the making of the court bouillon as part of the preparation of the dish itself, and you will find that you have made it before you realize that that's what you are doing. For the record, here is a recipe for court bouillon, which is very handy to have for poaching fish, among other things. If you omit the fish, you have a plain, ordinary court bouillon which can be used as a base for many sauces.

## COURT BOUILLON

2  *quarts water*
1  *bay leaf*
1  *carrot, chopped*
1  *stalk celery with leaves, chopped*
1  *small onion stuck with 2 cloves*
½  *cup vinegar or 1 cup dry white wine*
1  *teaspoon salt*
10  *whole black peppercorns*
3  *pounds fish or fish scraps (bones, fins, head, tail, etc.)*
*Lemon juice*

Put the water in a heavy pot and add the bay leaf, carrot, celery, onion, vinegar or white wine, salt and peppercorns. Bring to a boil. Rub fish or fish scraps with lemon juice and plunge into boiling water. As soon as the water returns to a boil, turn it down to a simmer and cook until the vegetables are tender. Strain the broth and reserve. Eat the fish, if you used one, and throw everything else away. *Makes 2 quarts of broth.*

THE NEXT three dishes are usually classified as soups, although my opinion is that they are stews, and my dictionary says they can be either. However you feel in the matter, I think you will agree that a good chowder makes mighty fine eating on a cold winter's day, or a warm summer one, for that matter. The first of the recipes will jar you right out of that comfortable rocker in which you are sitting. It's a chowder with a twist, and, at one time, was served at one of our local restaurants. The chef who invented it has since departed for other pastures, but not before he gave us the name of his secret ingredient. Try it; it's downright delicious. (If you want a recipe for a standard New England clam chowder, see the chapter on STEWS FOR TWO.)

## CLAM CHOWDER WITH A TWIST

3 *ounces salt pork, washed and in very small cubes*
4 *cups clams, carefully washed (or canned chopped clams)*
1 *large onion, minced*
3 *tablespoons flour*
1 *10½-ounce can condensed pea soup*
1 *cup water*
2 *cups diced raw potatoes*
1 *bay leaf*
3 *tablespoons butter*
2 *cups hot milk*

Put cubed salt pork in stewpot over medium low flame

and sauté until pork scraps are well browned. (See Manhattan Clam Chowder for directions on steaming open clam shells.) Separate the hard parts of clams from soft parts, chop hard parts finely and reserve soft parts. Remove browned pork bits and reserve. Add chopped hard bits of clams and minced onion to the grease and sauté for about 5 minutes. Add flour and stir until well blended. Add pea soup and water. Add potatoes and bay leaf, cover tightly and simmer until potatoes are just cooked but still firm. Add reserved soft parts of clams and browned pork bits and butter. Simmer gently for 5 minutes. Add very hot milk. Remove bay leaf. Turn off fire and let stand for 5 to 10 minutes before serving. *Serves 6.*

MY HUSBAND and I happen to be partial to New England clam chowder, but if you feel otherwise, or are bored with the kind made with milk, here is a recipe for Manhattan clam chowder.

## MANHATTAN CLAM CHOWDER

*3 dozen scrubbed clams in shell (be sure shells are tightly sealed)*
*1 cup water*
*3 tablespoons butter*
*2 large onions, chopped*
*2 leeks, chopped*
*1 clove garlic, pressed*
*1½ pounds raw potatoes, diced*
*3 large tomatoes, peeled and chopped*
*2 medium green peppers, seeded and chopped*
*3 stalks celery with leaves, thinly sliced*
*Clam broth and enough water to make 8 cups*
*2 pinches thyme*
*¼ teaspoon marjoram*
*2 shakes Tabasco sauce*
*Salt to taste*

Spread out clams in a baking dish, add water and place in hot oven until all clam shells have popped open (10 to 15 minutes). Set clams and liquid aside. Melt butter in stewpot over medium heat, add onions and leeks and cook until lightly browned. Add garlic, potatoes, tomatoes, green peppers and celery. Add clam broth and enough water to make 8 cups. Dice hard parts of clams and add with soft parts. Cover and simmer for 40 minutes. Add thyme, marjoram and Tabasco sauce. Stir thoroughly, salt to taste and let simmer a few minutes before serving piping hot. *Serves 6 to 8*.

IF YOU are not on speaking terms with clams, you can make chowder out of almost any fish you can lay your hands on. The word "chowder," by the way, comes from a French word meaning pot or kettle, and is not related to the slang word, "chow," which is short for "chowchow" and refers to a Chinese dish of mixed, preserved fruit. Anyhow, you can substitute any filleted fish for the haddock, cod and bass in the following recipe and still have an excellent fish chowder. Don't try to substitute shellfish, however, as they require a slightly different technique (you might say that they are a different kettle of fish).

## SAVORY FISH CHOWDER

3  pints water
½  teaspoon (heaping) salt
2  bay leaves
Generous pinch thyme
3  tablespoons chopped parsley
½  large clove garlic
10  peppercorns
1  pound cod, 1 pound bass, 1 pound haddock (or 3 pounds any fish)

½ pound salt pork, finely cubed
2 large onions, sliced thin
3 stalks celery with leaves, thinly sliced
1½ cups chicken broth
1 heaping tablespoon flour
Enough butter to make beurre manié
2 medium potatoes, diced
3 cups light cream
Salt and pepper to taste
½ cup dry sherry

Put water in stewpot over high flame, add salt, bay leaves, thyme, parsley, garlic and peppercorns. Bring to a simmer and add fish. Cover and simmer 10 minutes. Strain off broth and reserve. Skin and bone the fish, break into small pieces and set aside. Turn heat to medium under stewpot and fry salt pork until lightly browned. Remove bits of pork and reserve. Lower heat and gently sauté onions and celery 10 minutes. Add chicken broth mixed with reserved fish broth, and when the broth boils, drop in small balls of flour mixed with butter (*beurre manié*). Add diced potatoes and bits of pork. Simmer until potatoes are just tender (about 10 minutes), add cream and pieces of cooked fish. Salt and pepper to taste. Simmer another 10 minutes, add sherry and serve at once. *Serves 8.*

I GREW UP in the Rocky Mountains and therefore had little acquaintance with salt-water fish, other than shrimp, until I fled hearth and home for the inclemencies of New York City at a relatively tender age. There I was introduced to the oyster and found that I was one of those who could not bring her teeth together over this delicacy, much less swallow it whole. This aversion is still with me; I can eat fried oysters, oysters in a hangtown fry and smoked oysters, but spare me, please, the fresh, raw oyster. I also love oysters in oyster stew, and the following is the greatest.

# GOURMET OYSTER STEW

3  tablespoons butter
3  medium onions, minced
1  quart light cream
2  tablespoons chopped chives, fresh or frozen
2  bay leaves
1  pinch thyme
1½  quarts whole, raw oysters
½  cup sake or dry white wine
½  cup water
1  teaspoon salt
Paprika

Put butter in top of a double boiler and place directly over medium heat. Add onions and brown lightly. Have a small amount of water boiling gently in the bottom of double boiler, and when onions are brown, move top part over boiling water. Add cream, chives, bay leaves and thyme. Chop up 1 pint of oysters and add to cream mixture. Let water simmer gently for 20 minutes. Strain and return liquid to top of double boiler. Put the remaining quart of whole oysters in a saucepan with the sake and water and salt. Cook gently until the edges of the oysters begin to curl up, then add to the cream mixture and blend thoroughly. Dust each bowlful of chowder with paprika. *Serves 6.*

For the purpose of a stew, crab meat is one of the most versatile of sea foods. It does not mind being cooked a little extra time, and it thrives in a can. True, it is fairly costly, unless you are able to get it fresh, locally, but the fact that a dish is called a stew does not mean it must be made with inexpensive ingredients. In fact, the following dish is outstanding for its simplicity and elegance, and you may well decide to adopt it as a standby.

## CRAB MEAT STEWED IN MILK

3 tablespoons butter
1 large onion, minced
2 cups cooked crab meat, shredded
2 tablespoons flour
4 cups light cream
1½ cups cooked corn, shaved from cob
1 cup cubed artichoke hearts
Salt and pepper to taste
3 shakes Tabasco sauce
¼ cup Madeira

Melt butter over medium heat in stewpot and add onion. Sauté until onion begins to brown, then add crab meat and stir until thoroughly heated. Shake in flour while continuing to stir, then slowly add cream, stirring until smooth. Add corn, artichoke hearts, salt and pepper to taste and Tabasco sauce. Let simmer for 10 minutes. Remove from heat and add Madeira. Serve at once. *Serves 6.*

THE FOLLOWING RECIPE looks more like a stew, what with its green pepper, onion and mushrooms. It is also one of those that you can fiddle around with to suit your family's preferences, without doing any great harm to the basic idea, which is that these ingredients, in some combination, taste good when cooked together. So, if you like onions and don't much care for mushrooms, use more onions and fewer mushrooms than the recipe calls for. But try it the way it's written first; otherwise, you won't know whether what you've done is an improvement.

# CRAB MEAT STEWED WITH MUSHROOMS

6  tablespoons butter
1½  pounds cooked crab meat
2  medium green peppers, seeded and chopped
2  small onions, thinly sliced
3  small tomatoes, skinned and chopped
1  cup sliced mushrooms
1  clove garlic, pressed
½  cup sake or dry white wine
1  can chicken broth
Salt and pepper to taste

Melt butter in stewpot over medium heat, add crab meat, green pepper and onions. Lower heat and sauté gently until onions are tender. Add tomatoes, mushrooms, garlic, sake and chicken broth. Season to taste and let simmer for 15 minutes. *Serves 4.*

SHRIMP come in an assortment of sizes to suit almost any position on the menu except dessert, ranging from the teensy-weensy shrimp that are good for salads to the giant scampi, which are almost unobtainable in this country. The little-bitty shrimp are okay when found in cans, but, for most eating purposes, you should buy fresh shrimp or quick-frozen, *raw* shrimp, even though this means you will have to spend some time cleaning and shelling them. If you buy cooked shrimp, unless you get them from a reputable fish dealer who knows what he's doing, you are likely to have over-cooked or tasteless shrimp by the time they get to the table. Shrimp should be cooked only until they turn pink, a matter of about 5 minutes. They can be cooked before or after shelling, but if you cook them before you shell them, add a bay leaf, some peppercorns, ¼ or ½ lemon, a couple of cloves, ½ or ¾ cup dry white wine to the water, and you will have—Eureka!—a court bouillon. Otherwise, all you'll have is a mound of shrimp shells.

The following recipe is a good example of how to make a court bouillon and then use it in preparation of the stew. This is a Penang curry, so called for the island of that name near Singapore. Penang curries are famous for being hot, but a great deal depends upon the kind of curry powder used. If your curry powder has been sitting on a shelf for six months, it won't make anything taste very hot, so go out and buy a new supply, which, even if it has been sitting on the grocer's shelf for six months, has the advantage of never having been opened.

## SHRIMP CURRY

    2  cups water
    ½  cup sake or dry white wine
    1  bay leaf
    10  peppercorns
    ¼  lemon, squeezed gently
    6  whole cloves
    1  carrot, in 3 or 4 pieces
    1  onion, quartered
    2  pounds fresh shrimp (in the shell)
    ¼  pound butter
    2  medium onions, chopped
    2  stalks celery with leaves, chopped
    1  apple, peeled, cored and sliced
    2  small carrots, thinly sliced
    1  large tomato, peeled and chopped
    1½  tablespoons chopped parsley
    2  pinches dried mint
    ¼  teaspoon powdered cloves
    1  pinch thyme
    ½  teaspoon salt
    ¼  teaspoon nutmeg
    2  tablespoons flour

2  *tablespoons curry powder*
½  *cup sake or dry white wine*

Combine water, ½ cup sake, bay leaf, peppercorns, lemon, cloves, carrot and onion in stewpot and bring to boil. Add shrimp and simmer until they turn pink. Reserve liquid, which is court bouillon, and shell and devein shrimp. Put butter in pot over medium heat, add onions, celery, apple, carrots, tomato, parsley, mint, cloves, thyme, salt and nutmeg. Sauté gently until onions are tender. Mix flour and curry powder thoroughly and shake into the pot, stirring constantly until blended. Continue stirring and cook 5 minutes. Slowly add the reserved court bouillon while stirring, and then add the other ½ cup sake (with more water, if needed). Add shrimp and serve over rice with chutney on the side. *Serves 6.*


THE FLAVOR of some foods is as fragile as porcelain and should be handled with as great a respect. Shrimp fall into this category. Care must be taken that they not be overcooked, as they then become tasteless, which is especially disastrous if the shrimp are to be used in a stew. If the shrimp are overcooked, the stew will taste like celery-flavored water with oddly shaped lumps in it. Thus it is that many recipes using shrimp ask the cook to put the raw shrimp into the pot at the very end of the cooking time, so as not to risk overcooking. The following recipe is a tasty case in point.

## SHRIMP AND ARTICHOKE STEW

2  *tablespoons butter*
2  *tablespoons olive oil*
½  *cup chopped green pepper*
½  *cup chopped scallions*
2  *cloves garlic, pressed*

1 large can (preferably Italian) tomatoes
1½ teaspoons orégano
1 teaspoon basil
2 pinches powdered saffron
2 teaspoons salt
½ teaspoon sugar
⅓ cup sliced stuffed olives
½ cup sake or dry white wine
1 package frozen artichoke hearts (partly thawed)
1 pound shelled and deveined raw shrimp, in bite-size pieces
1 tablespoon water
1 tablespoon arrowroot

Melt butter and oil together in stewpot. Add green pepper and scallions and sauté until almost tender. Then add pressed garlic and cook until tender. Add tomatoes, orégano, basil, saffron, salt, sugar, olives and wine. Simmer very gently for 20 minutes. Add artichokes and shrimp and continue simmering until artichokes are tender, about 10 minutes. Mix arrowroot and water thoroughly and add, stirring until mixture thickens. *Serves 4.*

SHRIMP CREOLE is one of those dishes for which recipes abound, each one being slightly different from the other. The one chosen for this cookbook is unusual, if you will run your eye down the list of ingredients, in that it calls for tuna fish. This dish not only tastes good, it also looks pretty, with its bright green pepper and red tomatoes. Watch the cooking times here, as you don't want to overcook the shrimp *or* the green pepper, allowing the latter to remain crispy.

## SHRIMP CREOLE

2 tablespoons butter

½ cup chopped onion
2 stalks celery, thinly sliced
1½ pounds shelled and deveined raw shrimp, halved
   lengthwise
2 medium tomatoes, skinned and chopped
½ cup barbecue sauce
1 green pepper, seeded and chopped
1 7-ounce can tuna fish
¼ cup water
1 tablespoon cornstarch
½ cup sake or dry white wine
1 tablespoon finely chopped parsley

Put butter in stewpot over medium heat. Add onion
and celery and sauté until tender but not brown. Add
shrimp and continue cooking 5 minutes, stirring now
and then. Add tomatoes, barbecue sauce, green pepper
and tuna fish. Gradually add water, a little at a time, to
cornstarch until mixture is smooth, and add to pot.
Bring to a good simmer and add sake. Cook 5 minutes
and serve, sprinkled with parsley. *Serves 6.*

GREEN PEPPER and tomatoes add their eye- and taste-
appeal to the following dish, too, in addition to the
surprise of slivered almonds. It is a dish with an orien-
tal flavor to it, in that it emphasizes the textures of the
ingredients and cooks only the barest minimum of time.
You can do all the necessary peeling, slicing and shelling hours or days in advance, and then assemble and
cook about 10 minutes before dinnertime. You'll have
a gourmet dinner in less time than it takes to heat
something out of the freezer!

### SHRIMP STEW WITH ALMONDS

1 ounce shredded coconut
1 cup milk

4 tablespoons butter
3 green onions with tops, finely sliced
2 small onions, chopped
1 green pepper, seeded and diced
3 medium tomatoes, peeled and sliced
1 pound shelled and deveined raw shrimp
1 teaspoon salt
¼ teaspoon white pepper
½ teaspoon thyme
½ teaspoon basil
½ cup almonds, blanched and slivered
2 tablespoons flour

Combine shredded coconut and milk and let stand overnight in refrigerator. Melt butter in stewpot over medium heat and sauté all of the onions 5 minutes Add green pepper, tomatoes, shrimp, salt, white pepper, thyme, basil and almonds. Let simmer for 3 or 4 minutes, then remove from heat. Mash coconut into milk and let stand until ready to use. Strain and discard coconut. Put flour in cup and add coconut milk slowly to form a paste without lumps, and gradually stir in remainder of coconut milk. Stir this into the shrimp mixture while still off heat, then bring to a simmer, stirring constantly. Serve at once. *Serves 6.*

THE FIRST TIME my husband and I made deviled shrimp, we put the mixture through a sieve at the point at which this recipe says to put it in a blender. It took about an hour of our time and a half day of our energy to accomplish this, but the result was so delicious that we decided it was well worth it. Putting the mixture in the blender gives you a slightly different texture than sieving, but it is no less good for being easier to make. If you have no blender, get some strong-armed man to push it through a sieve, and then feed him the deviled shrimp as a reward—he will have earned it! And, by the way, you will note that your friend, the court bouillon, is here again.

## DEVILED SHRIMP, SHANTY SHAYNE

*1 cup butter*
*2 large onions, chopped*
*4 leeks, chopped*
*1 shallot, chopped (optional)*
*1 clove garlic, pressed*
*4 tablespoons chopped chives, fresh or frozen*
*2 pounds fresh raw shrimp, unpeeled*
*2 cups sake or dry white wine*
*1 small can tomatoes, drained*
*2 tablespoons tomato paste*
*½ cup beef bouillon*
*2 tablespoons finely chopped parsley*
*1 teaspoon salt*
*¼ teaspoon Tabasco sauce*
*2 tablespoons sweet butter*

Melt 1 cup butter in stewpot over medium heat. Add onions, leeks and shallot, reduce heat and sauté gently for 5 minutes. Add garlic and chives and sauté another 5 minutes. Throw in shrimp and cook another 5 minutes, stirring constantly. Add sake and simmer 10 minutes. Remove shrimp from pot, add tomatoes and tomato paste and simmer 7 minutes. Pour contents of pot into blender and blend thoroughly. Return to pot, add bouillon and boil gently until reduced into a fairly thick sauce. Shell and devein shrimp, and add to thickened sauce with parsley. Add salt and Tabasco sauce and bring to boil. Pour off at once into large serving bowl and allow sweet butter to melt on top before serving. *Serves 8.*

THE FIRST TIME I tried to cook a live lobster, I made

88

the mistake of letting it sit at the side of the stove while a pot of water was coming to a boil. This apparently alerted the lobster as to my plan for it, for, when I picked it up in order to put it in the pot, it fought back. We struggled for several seconds until I finally dropped it into the boiling water, clapped a lid over it and held it fast, feeling all the while as though I were murdering a small child. My husband tells me (and he is supported by various authorities) that the way to cook a live lobster is to put it in *cool* water that is then brought to a boil slowly and gently, so that the lobster succumbs with a smile on its face; this method supposedly results in more tender flesh. There is yet a third school which maintains that the lobster must be cut up while still alive, in order to preserve its full flavor, but, personally, I will have no part of such mayhem. If I must have anything to do with a live lobster (and, frankly, I prefer to let the fish market do the cooking), it is in cool water with that happy smile on its face. If you want to go around cutting up live lobsters, that's your business.

However you prepare the lobster for the following dish, the perfectionist would have you bring it home alive, and it is certainly true that the fresher a lobster is, the better it tastes. But this stew sauce is so marvelous that it would set off even canned lobster.

## FLAMED STEWED LOBSTER

*1 live lobster (1 to 2 pounds)*
*5 tablespoons cooking oil*
*1 heaping tablespoon butter*
*½ cup brandy or light rum*
*¼ teaspoon salt*
*¼ teaspoon paprika*
*½ cup sake or dry white wine*
*½ cup water*
*1 tablespoon tomato paste*
*3 green onions with tops, thinly sliced*

1 small clove garlic, pressed
2 medium tomatoes, peeled and chopped
1 teaspoon chervil
1 teaspoon rosemary
1 tablespoon tomato paste
2 teaspoons Bovril meat extract
1 tablespoon sweet butter

You can do this yourself or have the fish market do it. Split the live lobster, remove the coral, discard the sac and chop the tail and claws into pieces, leaving the shell in place. Heat the cooking oil in your stewpot until it is very hot but not smoking. Drop in the pieces of lobster and keep heat at high until shells are red (about 10 minutes). Remove pieces of lobster and pour off oil. Put butter in pot, lower heat and add lobster when butter is melted. Add brandy or rum and set it afire at once. Shake pieces of lobster in flame for 30 seconds, then cover to extinguish flame. Add salt, paprika, sake, water, tomato paste, onions, garlic, tomatoes, chervil and rosemary. Cover and simmer 35 minutes. While it is simmering, mash together the coral of the lobster with tomato paste, meat extract and sweet butter. When lobster is cooked, remove pieces to the bowl in which it is to be served, leaving sauce in pot over low heat. Add coral mixture gradually, while stirring, and simmer a couple of minutes. Strain the sauce over pieces of lobster and serve at once. *Serves 4.*

So MUCH for shellfish, which take more kindly to stewing than do other types of fish because at least they do not disintegrate in the stewpot. The following stews use just plain "fish," which means sole, halibut, flounder or any other ocean or fresh-water flatfish with white meat. These fish stews offer very tasty alternatives to sautéing, baking and poaching.

# FISH STEWED WITH NOODLES

3 cups chicken bouillon
1 pound tiny whole carrots, scraped
½ teaspoon caraway seed
1 teaspoon salt
2 teaspoons paprika
1 package frozen baby lima beans
1½ pounds fresh fish, filleted
½ pound egg noodles
½ cup flour
1 cup milk
2 teaspoons finely chopped parsley

Put bouillon in stewpot and bring to boil. Add carrots, caraway seed, salt, paprika, lima beans and fish. Cover and simmer until carrots are tender (about 12 minutes). While the above is simmering, cook noodles according to directions on package and drain. Put flour in small bowl, add milk gradually to make a paste without lumps, finally stirring in all the milk. When the carrots are tender, add drained noodles and flour mixture to the pot and simmer very gently for 10 minutes. Sprinkle parsley over top and serve. *Serves 4 to 6.*

# FISH STEWED WITH VEGETABLES

5 tablespoons butter
1 small onion, sliced
3 tablespoons tomato paste
2 pounds fresh fish, filleted
3 cups chicken broth
1 teaspoon salt
3 medium carrots, sliced
2 medium yams or sweet potatoes, cubed
1 package frozen okra

Melt butter in stewpot over medium heat, add onion

and sauté until onion is lightly browned. Add tomato paste and fish, cover and simmer very gently for 20 minutes. Add chicken broth, salt, carrots, yams and okra. Cover and simmer very gently until carrots and yams are tender (30 to 40 minutes). Add water if needed. *Serves 4 to 6.*

## FISH STEWED WITH RICE

2  8-ounce cans tomato sauce
1  medium onion, thinly sliced
¼  teaspoon Tabasco sauce
¼  pound butter
1  teaspoon salt
2  pounds fresh fish, filleted
1  package frozen okra
1  small head cabbage, coarsely grated
1  package frozen tiny peas
4  carrots, sliced
1  cup raw rice

Combine all ingredients except rice in stewpot and simmer gently for 10 minutes. Remove pieces of fish carefully to keep them whole, and set aside. Add rice and simmer until rice is cooked (about 30 to 40 minutes), adding water if needed to keep from sticking. Return pieces of fish to mixture and let heat 2 minutes before serving. *Serves 8.*

BOUILLABAISSE *sounds* so intimidating that few of us are intrepid enough to attempt to make it with our own pink hands at home. Actually, it isn't all that difficult; the most intimidating aspect of it is the number of different kinds of fish required to make it. Some authorities insist that it must contain at least five different kinds of fish in order to qualify as bouillabaisse. As you won't want to acquire all of these different sorts of fish just for a cozy little dinner for the family, plan to invite your more adventurous neighbors in to help sample the dish, or else organize some containers in which to freeze what you don't eat. Its flavor is every bit as marvelous on reheating, perhaps more so.

## BOUILLABAISSE FOR TEN

5 cups water
1 cup sake or dry white wine
6 whole cloves
1 teaspoon salt
2 pounds raw shrimp, unpeeled
2 tablespoons butter
2 large onions, chopped
2 cloves garlic, pressed
1 can tomato soup, condensed
1 cup chicken broth
4 whole cloves
2 bay leaves
2 teaspoons curry powder
½ pound American cheese, chopped
¼ cup sake or dry white wine
1½ pounds scallops
½ pound each of 4 different kinds of fish, filleted
½ pound mushrooms, sliced
2 tablespoons flour
Enough soft butter to moisten flour and form into balls
1 pound lobster meat, cooked and cubed
18 oysters

Put water and 1 cup sake in large saucepan, bring to boil and add cloves, salt and shrimp. Boil 8 minutes and set aside. Melt butter in stewpot, add onions and cook over medium heat until golden brown. Add garlic, tomato soup, chicken broth, cloves, bay leaves, curry powder, cheese and ¼ cup sake. Cover and simmer very slowly for 30 minutes. Remove shrimp from water (which is now a court bouillon), shell, devein and set aside. Bring court bouillon to a light boil, add scallops, four different kinds of fish and reduce heat to very slow simmer. Cover and simmer 15 minutes. Strain court bouillon from fish and set fish aside (you can throw the court bouillon away or save it for next time). By this time, the mixture in the stewpot should have simmered 30 minutes. Add halved shrimp and mushrooms to pot, and thicken with balls of flour and butter. Allow to simmer about 3 minutes to blend thoroughly, then throw in lobster meat and oysters and simmer another 3 minutes. Break fish into pieces and place on large platter and pour mixture from pot over the fish. *Serves 10.*

THERE ARE as many different ways to make bouillabaisse as there are to skin a cat. I hardly ever skin a cat, but I do make bouillabaisse, and it *is* possible to prepare it for fewer than ten people. The following recipe leaves the identities of the fish up to the maker of the stew, but it is customary to include at least two or three shellfish, because, as noted previously, they retain their individuality during the stewing process. (In buying shellfish, remember the rule of thumb that half the weight of the shellfish is in its shell. Thus, ½ pound of eating fish requires 1 pound of unshelled fish.)

## BOUILLABAISSE FOR SIX

¼  *pound butter*
2  *medium onions, thinly sliced*
1  *clove garlic, pressed*
1  *large tomato, peeled and sliced*
2  *bay leaves*
2  *cans tomato paste*

½ teaspoon saffron
½ cup chopped parsley
½ pound each of 4 different kinds of fish or shellfish
Enough water or court bouillon to cover
½ pound shrimp, cooked and cleaned
1 small can crab meat

Melt butter in stewpot over medium heat, add onions and lower heat to sauté 5 minutes. Add garlic and stir in well, then add tomato, bay leaves, tomato paste, saffron, parsley and fish or shellfish. Add enough water or court bouillon to cover and bring to boil quickly. Reduce heat to a good simmer and cook until fish are tender. Stir in shrimp and crab meat and let heat 2 minutes. *Serves 6.*

THE WORD "gumbo" belongs to Louisiana and derives from a Bantu word meaning okra. Consequently, any stew that uses okra as its primary thickening agent could be called a gumbo, although the term is usually reserved for those dishes that come to us from Louisiana, such as the following.

## SEAFOOD GUMBO

6 ounces salt pork, washed and diced
4 medium onions, chopped fine
1½ tablespoons flour
2 green peppers, chopped
3 teaspoons lemon juice
2 cloves garlic, pressed
3 bay leaves
1 teaspoon Worcestershire sauce
¼ teaspoon Tabasco sauce
¼ teaspoon rosemary
½ teaspoon thyme
1 teaspoon salt

3 packages frozen okra, sliced
3 pounds raw shrimp, peeled and deveined
1½ pounds fresh crab meat, shredded
24 oysters
1 can chicken broth (or more if needed)

Throw salt pork into stewpot over medium heat and cook until cubes are thoroughly browned. Remove pork scraps and retain. Add onions and reduce heat to lowest point. Cover and cook until brown and mushy (1 hour or more). Stir in flour until smooth, add bits of salt pork, green peppers, lemon juice, garlic, bay leaves, Worcestershire sauce, Tabasco sauce, rosemary, thyme, salt and okra. Simmer gently for 30 minutes. Add shrimp, crab meat, oysters and chicken broth (enough to make the mixture soupy). Boil gently for 20 minutes. *Serves 12.*

# 4

## STEWS AROUND THE WORLD

STEWS, as affirmed in the Introduction to this volume, are well nigh universal. Put down your knapsack unexpectedly on the doorstep in any cranny of the world, and chances are you'll find they are having stew for dinner. They may not call it that, and the stew may have an accent that you don't immediately recognize, but the basic cooking process will be stewing, and the end result is more than likely to be scrumptious.

Some of the most famous dishes in the world are stews, and I have tried to gather together in this chapter some representative samples of stewing as it is done in various parts of this shrinking world of ours. If people paid more attention to each other's cuisine and less to ideological beliefs, there might be less mayhem committed on an international scale. Cooking is a science and, like a science, knows no national boundaries.

On the other hand, world peace based upon a culinary exchange might not be such a good idea. It is true that one woman shows her respect for another by asking her for a recipe. So far, so good. But it is also true that it is extraordinarily difficult to record a prized recipe faithfully for a competitor. One is flattered by the request, but one is also likely to omit a primary ingredient or an essential step, and there goes your world peace! It takes no great imagination to envisage the arguments that might occur over the amount and type of curry powder required to make an *authentic* curry, or how much paprika to put in the Hungarian goulash. No, I think it would be unwise to substitute cooks for diplomats at the world's council tables, although one can't say that the diplomats are doing such a hot-shot job of it.

This chapter of the cookbook is intended for those of you who are adventurous, and even the most conservative of my readers must have adventurous days once in a while on which ordinary food won't do at all, and one must have mustacholi or hassenpfeffer. And what if your teen-age son will eat nothing but hamburgers or pizza? Let him munch on hamburgers while you dine on couscous or riganato or chicken cacciatore.

Some of these stews require days to prepare, and some of them ask for ingredients that may be hard for you to find, but that is part of the adventure. Some of them sound more difficult than they are, and some of them are more difficult than they sound. But don't cheat. Do everything the way it says to do it, and you will find each of these stews a richly rewarding experience.


PERHAPS some of the best-known and most elegantly disguised stews are French in origin. I found I had five French stews which were "musts" for this chapter, and two others which are included in the chapter called "Special Stews for Guests." The two French "guest" stews are variations on a theme, being different versions of coq au vin and boeuf bourguignonne than those included here. One thing one learns at the outset of reading and writing cookbooks is that there is no single authoritative recipe for anything, there is only a single authoritative recipe for the way so-and-so cooks it, and so-and-so could be a famous chef, your next-door neighbor or yourself. So, go ahead and make up your version of coq au vin and then call it coq au vin à la Jane Smith, or whatever your name is. But before you start inventing, try the following recipe, which is a favorite at our house and never fails.

## COQ AU VIN A LA SHANTY SHAYNE

¼ pound salt pork, washed and cubed
½ cup flour
1 teaspoon salt
½ teaspoon black pepper
Dash paprika
Dash nutmeg
2 broilers, disjointed
½ cup Calvados or other apple brandy
18 pearl onions, whole
2 cloves garlic, pressed
1 teaspoon fines herbes (chives, chervil and thyme)
2 teaspoons chopped parsley
2 tablespoons chopped celery leaves
1 cup sliced mushrooms
1 cup sake or dry white wine
1 cup good red burgundy

Put cubes of salt pork in stewpot over medium heat and cook to a crisp. Put flour, salt, pepper, paprika and nutmeg in paper bag, and shake pieces of chicken in this until thoroughly floured. Remove crisp bits of pork from pot and set aside. Place floured pieces of chicken in hot grease and brown on all sides. Turn off heat and add Calvados, set afire and shake pot until the flame goes out. Remove browned pieces of chicken and set aside. Turn heat to low, add reserved bits of pork, onions, garlic, fines herbes, parsley, celery leaves, mushrooms, and cook slowly, uncovered, 10 minutes, while stirring frequently. Add sake, burgundy and chicken. Cover and simmer very, very slowly for 1½ hours. *Serves 4.*

IN FRENCH COOKERY, one frequently bumps into the word *ragout* (pronounced *rah-goo*), which means stew and derives from the French word for restoring one's appetite. To call a stew a ragout adds a mystical quality to it, and that goes a long way toward restoring anybody's appetite. A ragout can be made out of almost anything, and frequently is, particularly at the local parlor-car-converted-into-a-diner. A student's ragout, by the way, is a stew made without any meat, on the assumption that students are usually poverty-stricken, an assumption that is no longer valid among today's affluent students. The following ragout is made with veal and is extra-delicious.

## VEAL RAGOUT

4 *tablespoons butter*
3 *pounds boned and cubed lean veal*
3 *large onions, thinly sliced*
4 *cloves garlic, pressed*
1 *teaspoon curry powder*
4 *cups water*
1 *cup sake*
1 *can tomato soup*
*About 1 tablespoon salt (to taste)*
½ *pound mushrooms, sliced*

Put butter in stewpot over high heat until it sizzles but does not smoke. Add veal and onions and lower heat to medium. Cook until onions are well browned, stirring as you go. Add garlic and stir in, then add curry powder, water, sake, tomato soup and salt to taste. Cover tightly and simmer very slowly for at least an hour. Add mushrooms and simmer another 10 minutes. *Serves 6.*

BOEUF BOURGUIGNONNE is a ragout the way it is prepared in Burgundy—and those Burgundians are hearty eaters as well as providers of some of the best wine you can buy. The following recipe takes a long time from beginning to end, but it deserves your tenderest loving care and close attention to detail. You may resent burning up that amount of cognac, but it really does make a difference in the flavor of the final result. Anything cooked this way just *has* to be good.

## BOEUF BOURGUIGNONNE (*Beef Burgundy*)

4 to 5 pounds boned and cubed beef shoulder
1 cup good wine vinegar
2 cups good red burgundy
½ cup sake or dry white wine
1 leek, sliced
2 stalks celery, sliced
2 small carrots, sliced
1 teaspoon fines herbes (chives, chervil and thyme)
1 teaspoon salt
¼ teaspoon red pepper
½ pound salt pork, washed
2 green peppers, seeded and sliced
2 cloves garlic
1 bay leaf
1 small bunch parsley (tied with string)
½ can jellied madrilene
1 cup pitted ripe olives, halved
4 ounces brandy or light rum
1 pound mushrooms, sliced

Dip the pieces of beef in vinegar and drain on paper towel. In a large bowl, put burgundy, sake, leek, celery, carrots, fines herbes, salt and red pepper. Add cubed beef to above mixture and marinate at least 12 hours, stirring occasionally to soak all pieces of beef. Remove meat to drain on paper towel. Strain off marinade and reserve. Dice salt pork and put in stewpot over medium heat, stirring constantly until all fat is cooked out. Remove crisp bits of pork with slotted spoon and brown cubes of marinaded beef in fat until lightly browned. Add green peppers and garlic during last few minutes, and pour in reserved marinade. Bring to boil and add bay leaf and parsley and bits of browned pork. Cover and simmer 3 hours (or until meat is nicely tender). Drain off liquid into bowl and turn off heat. Place liquid in freezing compartment of refrigerator until fat congeals on top. Remove fat and pour liquid over meat in stewpot and bring to boil. Add jellied madrilene, olives, and float brandy or rum on top. Set afire at once and wait until flame goes out. Add mushrooms and simmer 30 minutes. Remove bay leaf and bunch of parsley and serve. *Serves 8.*

IF YOU THINK that French cooking is based upon wine and butter and a clever imagination, you are right—but only up to a point. The cassoulet is a French stew that is not only famous and inexpensive, but is also based upon dry beans. It gets its name from the casserole-type vessel in which it was originally cooked, but it is really a stew and, in the following recipe, is cooked on top of the stove. Strictly speaking, it should be made with white beans, but if you have an aversion to white beans, use red or pinto beans, which will do just as well. It will still be a cassoulet and still be delicious.

## CASSOULET

½  *pound dry beans*
1  *quart water*
1  *bay leaf, crushed*
3  *onions, thickly sliced*
1  *teaspoon chili powder*

4 lamb shoulder chops
½ pound link sausages, halved
1 clove garlic, pressed
¼ pound salt pork, washed and cubed
½ cup sake or dry white wine
Salt to taste

Soak beans several hours or overnight in stewpot with water. Drain off any excess water to leave beans well covered. Stir in bay leaf, onions and chili powder. Trim fat from chops and drop into heavy frying pan over medium-high heat to reduce to cracklings .Cut chops in thirds or quarters (retaining bones). When bits of fat are crisp, remove with slotted spoon and add to bean pot. Brown pieces of chops on both sides and add to pot. Brown halved sausages and add to pot. Add garlic, salt pork and sake. Season to taste with salt. Simmer 1½ hours. *Serves 6.*

ANOTHER very famous French stew is boeuf en daube, so-called because of the pot, called a *daubière,* in which it was originally cooked. It is the mainstay of much of French cooking, particularly in the southern part. The *daubière* is a closed earthenware pot, which is buried in hot cinders for a very long time, so that the stew can cook away merrily, untended by any eye but God's. If you've never tried to cook anything in a pot buried in hot cinders, you will be highly skeptical as to the efficiency of this method of cooking. One interesting feature of the *daube* is that it is very good served cold. Put the meat, after it is cooked, in a bowl and strain the juice over it. This will jell when you put it in the refrigerator, and the meat can then be sliced and served cold.

# BOEUF EN DAUBE

¼   pound salt pork, washed and cubed
2   tablespoons flour
1   teaspoon seasoned salt
3   pounds boned and cubed beef shoulder
2   cloves garlic, minced
¼   cup brandy or light rum
½   pound small mushrooms, sliced
1   can beef broth
1½  cups dry red wine
16  small pearl onions, whole
1   bunch tiny whole baby carrots, scraped
8   peppercorns
1   bay leaf, crumbled
6   whole cloves
1   tablespoon chopped parsley
½   teaspoon fines herbes (chives, chervil and thyme)
½   cup sake

Put salt pork in stewpot and brown lightly but not until crisp. Remove pork and reserve. Put flour and seasoned salt in a paper bag and shake cubed beef in it. Add beef and garlic to pork fat in pot over medium heat and sauté until very lightly browned. Add brandy or rum, light and let flame about 30 seconds before clapping on lid to extinguish flames. Add mushrooms, broth, red wine, onions and carrots. Tie peppercorns, bay leaf, cloves, parsley and fines herbes in a piece of cheesecloth and add to stew. Cover and simmer for 1½ hours. Add sake and simmer very gently for another ½ hour. Remove bag of herbs and serve. *Serves 8.*

THE ITALIANS go about stewing in quite a different way than do the French, at least insofar as their more well-known dishes are concerned. I was tempted to include a recipe for spaghetti and meatballs when I came to

this part of the cookbook, but finally had to admit—
reluctantly, you may be sure—that this was a sauce
rather than a stew. So, this cookbook includes only two
Italian stews, one of which (veal scaloppini) appears in
the chapter called "Special Stews for Guests." In this
chapter, in which we go wandering in and out of kitch-
ens all over the world, we have chicken cacciatore, one
of my favorite stews.

## CHICKEN CACCIATORE

½  cup olive oil (more as needed)
1  frying chicken, 3½ to 4 pounds, disjointed
½  teaspoon seasoned salt
4  onions, sliced
2  green peppers, seeded and sliced
2  cloves garlic, whole
1  large can tomato sauce

Heat olive oil in stewpot over medium heat. Lightly
season pieces of chicken with seasoned salt, and add to
hot oil and cover. Lower heat to slow simmer and cook
1 hour, turning occasionally. Remove chicken from pot
and add more olive oil, if needed. Add onions and
sauté for 15 minutes, then add green peppers and garlic
and sauté gently another 10 minutes. Remove cloves of
garlic, add tomato sauce and chicken and simmer all
together for 15 minutes. *Serves 4.*

SPANISH COOKING is perhaps better known for its casseroles than for its stews. It saddened me that I could
think of no logical way in which to incorporate arroz
con pollo or paella into my stew cookbook, but it just
couldn't be done; you'll have to invest in another cookbook in order to get recipes for these two fascinating
dishes. Meanwhile, we have from Spain a mustacholi,

which is a fine, hearty stew with a good bite to it in the form of chili powder.

## MUSTACHOLI

1½ tablespoons olive oil
1½ pounds boned and cubed beef shank
3 medium onions, sliced
1 No. 2 can tomatoes
3 stalks celery with leaves, sliced
1 medium can pimientos
½ pound small whole mushrooms
1 teaspoon salt
¼ teaspoon cayenne pepper
1 to 2 tablespoons chili powder (to taste)

Heat oil in stewpot over medium heat, add cubed meat and onions and cook until onions are lightly browned (about 12 minutes). Add tomatoes, celery, pimientos, mushrooms, salt and pepper. Mix 1 tablespoon chili powder with enough olive oil to make a paste, and stir this into mixture first. Taste and add more chili powder if your taste buds call for it. Cover and simmer slowly for 1½ hours, or until meat is tender, adding water if necessary. *Serves 4.*

To CONTINUE with stews that have a hot bite to them, we must move to this hemisphere and south of the border. My husband grew up in West Texas, not too far from the Rio Grande, where he learned to make frijole con chili con carne the way it should be made —according to him. This means beans with chili with meat, and there was a time when you were considered to be pretty lucky to have any meat to put with your beans, even if it was only salt pork. If you want to start an argument with a cook from Texas, just question the *kind* of bean he uses in his frijoles. My husband maintains that the only bean to be used in an authentic chili is a red bean, but there are many who aver with equal vigor that the only bean to be used is the kidney bean. In restaurants, the kidney bean is usually served, but it is milder and larger than the red bean. For my part, the two groups can go on debating the matter all they want to, provided they continue cooking.

The following recipe takes the middle path in the matter of seasoning, being neither very hot nor very bland, insofar as the chili powder is concerned. You can tone it up or down depending upon your own taste.

## CHILI CON CARNE CON FRIJOLES, SHANTY SHAYNE

*1½  pounds red beans (frijoles)*
*Enough water to cover with an inch over top of beans*
*1  teaspoon baking soda*
*1  pound fat salt pork, washed and cubed*
*5  large onions, sliced*
*2  pounds ground beef, chuck or shoulder*
*½  cup flour*
*½  cup chili powder*
*1  tablespoon seasoned salt (or less, to taste)*
*Olive oil*
*1  can condensed tomato soup*

Soak beans in water in stewpot overnight. When ready to cook, add soda and water to cover well (if needed) and bring to a gentle boil. Put salt pork in heavy frying pan over moderate heat and cook, stirring frequently, until cubes of pork are light brown but not crisp. Remove pork with slotted spoon and add to bean pot. Measure off grease into cup, discarding any excess or adding butter to make a full cup if needed. Return to frying pan over moderate heat, add sliced onions and sauté until lightly browned. Add ground beef and continue cooking, mashing meat into the fat and onions with a two-tined fork and stirring constantly until ground meat is separated and free from lumps. After cooking about 20 minutes, mix flour, chili powder and seasoned salt in small bowl and add enough olive oil to moisten into a paste. Stir this mixture into bean pot, add tomato soup and check seasoning. Add ground meat and onion mixture. Turn to low simmer and continue cooking until beans have cooked at least 2 hours. Add water toward the last if you desire thinner sauce. *Serves 8.*

THE FOREGOING chili dish originated in Mexico, rather than Texas (although one would never guess this from the way some Texans talk), where chili is as essential to cookery as salt. One finds highly spiced cooking in all hot, southern countries, and the reason for this is not very romantic. Strong seasonings are used lavishly in order to cover the taste of meat that has been hanging in the sun a little too long. Fortunately, over-aged meat is not essential to the successful outcome of the dish; the following recipe works perfectly well with a nice, fresh chicken right out of your butcher's refrigerator. The chocolate gives this dish a very distinctive flavor.

## MEXICAN CHICKEN

*1 roasting chicken, 5 pounds, disjointed*
*1 teaspoon salt*
*3 cups water*
*5 tablespoons olive oil*
*1 large onion, sliced*
*1 small can sliced pimientos*
*1 medium can tomatoes*
*2 cloves garlic, crushed*
*Olive oil*

2 (or more) tablespoons chili powder
Chicken broth (if needed)
⅓ cup ground peanuts
⅓ cup ground almonds
½ teaspoon aniseed
3 ounces seeded raisins, chopped
¼ teaspoon nutmeg
Grated rind 1 orange
1 pinch powdered cloves
2 pinches cinnamon
2 dashes Tabasco sauce
1 square bitter chocolate, grated

Put chicken in stewpot with salt and water to cover well. Bring to a nice simmer, cover and cook for 40 minutes. Set pieces of chicken aside and reserve broth. Heat olive oil in stewpot and add onion, pimientos, tomatoes and garlic, and sauté for 15 minutes. Mix enough olive oil with chili powder to make a paste, and stir in with the vegetables. Measure the broth you have reserved and add canned chicken broth if needed to make 2½ cups. Add this to pot and bring to boil, then add peanuts, almonds, aniseed, raisins, nutmeg, orange rind, cloves, cinnamon and Tabasco sauce. Cover pot and simmer gently for 30 minutes, stirring occasionally. Stir in grated chocolate, add chicken to the mixture and heat for 10 minutes. *Serves 6.*

NEAR MEXICO is the Caribbean Sea, and one would hope to get a romantic stew from at least one of those islands full of sunshine, sand, calypso singers and rum punches. However, the only Caribbean stew with which I have any acquaintance is one called ropa vieja, which sounds as though it means "old rope" (and maybe it does), roughly translated as "raggedy beef." Not very romantic, and about the only exotic ingredient in the stew is pimiento and not much of that. However, it is quite tasty and unusual, in spite of the apparently mundane nature of the contents.

## ROPA VIEJA (*Raggedy Beef Stew*)

3  pounds boned beef shank, cut in 1-inch cubes
¼  pound salt pork, washed and diced
1  medium onion, sliced
2  bay leaves
2  carrots, sliced
Water to cover
2  tablespoons butter
1  large onion, diced
2  cloves garlic, pressed
2  pounds tomatoes, peeled, quartered and seeded
3  whole cloves
1½  teaspoons salt (or more to taste)
¼  teaspoon cayenne pepper
1½  teaspoons paprika
3  slices white bread, torn into bits
2  small cans sliced pimientos

Put meat, salt pork, onion, bay leaves and carrots in stewpot, cover with water and bring to gentle simmer. Cover and cook gently 3 to 4 hours, until meat separates into shreds easily. Remove meat and pour off broth and reserve. Melt butter in pot over moderate heat, add onion and sauté 12 minutes. Add garlic, tomatoes, cloves, salt, cayenne pepper and paprika, and sauté another 10 minutes. While these vegetables are cooking, separate the meat into shreds and have ready to add later. At the end of 10 minutes, pour reserved meat broth over sautéed vegetables and bring to light boil. Add bread and stir until dissolved and absorbed, then add shredded meat and pimientos. *Serves 6.*

BACK TO EUROPE, we encounter one of the most famous stews of the Western world and one of the most often insulted on the menus of diners from New York to the Yukon: Hungarian goulash. Hungarians, as a group, are a charming people, exuberant and optimistic, and Hungarian goulash ought to partake of some of these qualities, instead of which, it is frequently sodden, gray and greasy. On the other hand, it seems to be impossible to discover an authoritative recipe for goulash, probably because it, like so many other stews, is made with whatever is available. Herewith are two recipes for Hungarian goulash, one with beef and one with veal, but it can also be made with pork and, I suppose, lamb. You pays your money and you takes your choice.

## HUNGARIAN GOULASH WITH BEEF

- *4 tablespoons butter*
- *2 large onions (red preferred) sliced thin*
- *2½ pounds lean round steak, cubed*
- *1 tablespoon paprika*
- *½ cup tomato sauce*
- *¼ teaspoon aniseed*
- *½ teaspoon fines herbes (parsley, chives, chervil and thyme)*
- *½ cup good red burgundy*
- *½ cup beef bouillon*
- *Salt to taste*
- *4 medium potatoes, peeled and cubed*
- *1 tablespoon butter*
- *½ teaspoon (heaping) paprika*
- *1 tablespoon warm sake or dry white wine*

Melt 4 tablespoons butter in stewpot over medium heat, add onions and sauté until just tender. Add meat and continue cooking over lower heat, stirring frequently, until onions are brown. Add 1 tablespoon paprika, tomato sauce, aniseed, fines herbes, wine and bouillon. Cover pot and simmer very gently for about 2 hours, until meat is just tender but not quite done, adding a mixture of ½ wine, ½ water, if needed while cooking. Salt to taste. Now add the potatoes and cook about 30 minutes until they are tender. Just before serving, melt 1 tablespoon butter and stir in the heaping ½ teaspoon of paprika and warm sake. Pour into pot and give one quick stirring, then serve. *Serves 6.*

MY HUSBAND and I once had as a house guest a Hungarian musician who spoke no English, and as we speak no Hungarian, there would have been a communication problem, had not the musician been traveling with a friend who knew both languages. On about the third day of his visit with us, he announced that he would reward our hospitality by making for us a paprikash salad. We, of course, were enormously curious as to what a genuine Hungarian would call a "paprikash salad," and I had visions of a green salad tossed in vinegar and oil and ground paprika. Nothing could have been further from the truth. Our Hungarian friend put about twelve large green bell peppers into a hot oven, where they roasted until the thin outer skin was brown and cracked. Then he peeled them, cut them into strips and tossed them in a dressing made from oil, salt, pepper and an entire head of garlic, finely minced. Not only was there no paprika in the salad, but it should have been named for the garlic, for I could taste only the garlic for weeks afterward, and the house had to be aired for days to get rid of the smell.

I don't know if all Hungarians use garlic this lavishly in their cooking; I don't see how they could do it and remain as charming as they are. The following recipe for Hungarian goulash with dumplings uses garlic more sanely.

# HUNGARIAN GOULASH WITH VEAL AND DUMPLINGS

2 tablespoons butter
2 tablespoons flour
1 teaspoon seasoned salt
2½ pounds veal, cut into ½-inch cubes
1 tablespoon paprika
1 medium onion, sliced
½ cup chicken broth
½ cup sake or dry white wine
1 clove garlic, pressed

DUMPLINGS

1¼ cups flour
½ teaspoon salt
3 heaping teaspoons double-action baking powder
⅔ cup milk (or less, if possible)

Put butter in stewpot over moderate heat. Put flour and seasoned salt in paper bag and shake veal in this mixture until each cube is thoroughly coated. Add veal and paprika and cook over medium heat until meat is well browned. Reduce heat, add onion, chicken broth, sake and garlic. Cover pot and simmer very slowly for 30 minutes, or until meat is just tender. To make the dumplings, sift flour, salt and baking powder into a bowl and stir milk in slowly. The trick to getting fluffy dumplings is to use as little milk as possible to form a dough that can just be stirred. Drop by heaping teaspoonfuls on top of meat in pot, cover and boil gently for 20 minutes. *Serves 4 to 6.*

ANOTHER FAMOUS STEW from Europe is sauerbraten, which many cooks find intimidating, although I do not understand why. Perhaps it's the long marination, but that isn't work, it's simply a matter of buying the meat far enough in advance to allow time for the marinating. Admittedly, it is difficult on Monday to consider what may happen on Thursday, so don't think about sauerbraten on Monday. Wait until Tuesday or Wednesday and then consider sauerbraten for the weekend, a much happier pair of days to think about.

## SAUERBRATEN

4-pound rump roast
1 cup good red wine
½ cup sake or dry white wine
½ cup water
¾ cup tarragon or wine vinegar
3 bay leaves
3 medium onions, sliced
2 carrots, sliced
1 stalk celery with leaves, sliced
10 cloves
1 teaspoon dry mustard
12 peppercorns
2 cloves garlic, peeled and quartered
1 teaspoon salt
1 teaspoon fines herbes (parsley, chives, chevril and thyme)
¼ teaspoon nutmeg
3 tablespoons butter
2 tablespoons flour
6 gingersnaps
1 cup sour cream

Put rump roast in a large pot in which it can be turned easily, and add red wine, sake, water, vinegar, bay leaves, onions, carrots, celery, cloves, mustard, peppercorns, garlic, salt, fines herbes and nutmeg as a marinade. Marinate for at least 2 days (3 or 4 are better),

114

putting in refrigerator at night and removing during day to sit at room temperature while you turn the meat in the mixture several times. Put butter in stewpot and melt over moderate heat. Remove roast from marinade and brown it on all sides in the butter. Remove meat and lower heat to blend in flour and crushed ginger-snaps. Slowly pour in the marinade, stirring as you go, then add roast, cover and simmer about 3 hours, until meat is very tender. Add a mixture of ½ water and ½ sake if needed while cooking to keep sauce at the right consistency. When meat is tender, remove to a warm platter and slice. Strain sauce. Add sour cream to sauce and bring just to a simmer, then pour over slices of meat. *Serves 8.*

THE DIRECTIONS for cooking hasenpfeffer are very similar to those for cooking sauerbraten; in fact, you could substitute rabbit for beef in the foregoing and the result would be hasenpfeffer. By the same token, the following recipe for hasenpfeffer would also work for sauerbraten by substituting beef for rabbit. This one is a little less complicated and calls for fewer herbs.

## HASENPFEFFER

*1  large or 2 small rabbits, disjointed*
*1  cup burgundy*
*½  cup sake or dry white wine*
*1½  cups water*
*½  cup wine vinegar*
*4  bay leaves*
*2  medium onions, sliced*
*1  tablespoon chopped parsley*
*Leaves from 6 stalks of celery, chopped*
*1  tablespoon salt*
*8  peppercorns*
*1  tablespoon lemon juice*

*3 tablespoons butter*
*2 tablespoons flour*
*6 gingersnaps*
*½ cup sour cream*

Place rabbit in a container that holds at least 3 quarts, and add burgundy, sake, water, vinegar, bay leaves, onions, parsley, celery leaves, salt, peppercorns and lemon juice. Marinate 2 or 3 days in refrigerator. Put butter in stewpot over medium heat and brown the pieces of rabbit thoroughly on all sides. Remove rabbit and blend in flour (adding more butter if needed) and crushed gingersnaps. Pour in the marinade and add browned rabbit, cover and simmer very gently about 2 hours, until rabbit is tender. Remove rabbit to warm platter and strain the sauce, returning strained sauce to pot. Stir in sour cream and bring to simmer. Pour sauce over pieces of rabbit. *Serves 6.*

ANOTHER DISH that requires a long period of marination is the following Portuguese pot roast. It is not spicy, as sauerbraten is, and the flavor of the wine in which it is marinated remains as a haunting memory of something altogether pleasant. Remember when selecting the wine to use in a marinade that a dish is only as good as its ingredients, and a cheap wine that is not good enough for drinking is not good enough for cooking, either.

## PORTUGUESE POT ROAST

*4-pound rump roast*
*1 cup good red wine*
*½ cup sake or dry white wine*
*½ cup water*
*3 large onions, sliced*
*2 teaspoons salt*

6  *peppercorns*
4  *whole cloves*
4  *tablespoons butter*
2  *tomatoes, peeled and quartered*
*Instant flour*

Place roast in a pot large enough for it to be turned easily, add red wine, sake, water, onions, salt, peppercorns and cloves. Marinate 2 days, leaving in refrigerator at night and leaving out during days so it can be turned occasionally. Remove from marinade and dry thoroughly. Put butter in stewpot over medium heat, and brown roast on all sides. Pour in marinade and add water (if needed) to bring liquid up almost to top of roast. Cover and simmer for 2½ hours, then add tomatoes and begin testing roast with a fork. Cook for another ½ to 1 hour (be careful not to overcook), until meat is nicely tender. Remove from pot to warm platter and slice. Strain the sauce and return to pot and let sit a few minutes without heat before shaking in enough instant flour to thicken, stirring vigorously as you do so. After flour is blended, bring to a simmer for a few minutes before pouring over sliced roast. *Serves 8.*

IF YOU TRY to pronounce the name of the following dish, it will sound like a sneeze, so you might just as well take the easy path and call it a Swiss stew, as that is what it is. The important thing to watch is to cut the meat into very small pieces, as if you were preparing it for a family of toothless old gentlemen. This is rather a refreshing change from the big chunks one usually finds in stews.

### GESCHNETZELTES *(Swiss Stew)*

4  *tablespoons butter*
2  *large onions, diced*

2 *tablespoons chopped parsley*
1 *tablespoon flour*
½ *pound round steak, in ½-inch cubes*
½ *pound veal, in ½-inch cubes*
½ *pound lean lamb, in ½-inch cubes*
½ *cup sake or dry white wine*
*Salt and pepper to taste*

Melt butter in stewpot over moderate heat, add onions and parsley and sauté slowly for 10 minutes, stirring frequently. Add flour and blend well, then drop in the cubes of meat and turn heat quite high for 2 or 3 minutes, stirring constantly. Reduce heat to very low and wait 5 minutes before adding sake. Cover and simmer 40 minutes to 1 hour, until meat is very tender. Season to taste. *Serves 4.*

ONE FINAL WORD from the continent of Europe is the following stew from Poland. It is called a hunter's stew, and one can only speculate that Polish hunters have enormous appetites and carry with them a larger assortment of cooking ingredients than do most hunters. Or perhaps they borrow from the nearest farm. Wherever the materials come from, the resultant stew is a hearty brew indeed and just begs to be ladled out on one of those crispy fall or winter days that seems to be made for a good stew.

### BIGOS (Hunter's Stew)

2 *tablespoons butter*
1 *large onion, chopped*
1 *can beef broth*
2 *pounds Polish sausage, diced*
1 *small head cabbage, shredded*
1 *cup sliced mushrooms*
3 *cups sauerkraut*

1  *can tomato sauce*
2  *apples, peeled and diced*
½  *cup pitted prunes, quartered*
1  *teaspoon salt*
*Freshly ground pepper to taste*
½  *cup good red wine*
¼  *cup water*
1  *clove garlic, pressed*

Melt butter in stewpot and sauté onion until lightly browned. Add broth, sausage, cabbage, mushrooms, sauerkraut, tomato sauce, apples, prunes, salt and pepper. Cover and simmer very slowly 1½ hours. Add wine, water and garlic, and simmer another 40 minutes. If any is left over, it should be stored in the refrigerator in a glass bowl. *Serves 8.*

THE USE of eggplant and tomato together in a stew seems to belong to the Near East, as will be noted in several of the following recipes coming from countries this side of the Orient. In the Greek lamb stew immediately below, the eggplant actually acts as a thickening agent, for it cooks into mush which permeates the entire stew with the very faintest of flavors. This stew is particularly good on reheating, when you should mix the cooked macaroni into the stew instead of serving it separately.

## GREEK LAMB STEW

4  *tablespoons olive oil*
3½  *pounds boned leg of lamb, cubed*
3  *medium onions, sliced*
2  *cans tomato sauce*
¼  *cup water*
1  *teaspoon salt*
1  *teaspoon marjoram*

¼ teaspoon freshly ground pepper
1 medium eggplant, cubed
2 green peppers, seeded and diced
1 package frozen okra
3 medium tomatoes, peeled and quartered
3 cups elbow macaroni

Heat olive oil in stewpot and brown the pieces of lamb on all sides. Add onions and sauté gently about 10 minutes. Add tomato sauce, water, salt, marjoram and pepper. Cover and simmer 45 minutes, then add eggplant, peppers and okra, and simmer another 30 minutes or until lamb is tender. Add tomatoes and cook about 7 minutes, uncovered, stirring occasionally. Cook macaroni as directed on package, drain and put in large serving bowl. Pour the stew over it to serve. *Serves 8.*

ANOTHER STEW from Greece capitalizes on the affinity that lamb has for orégano. And a word of caution, please. If your orégano has been standing around on your spice shelf for several years, or even months, throw it away and get a new batch. Dried herbs lose their gumption in a very short time after the container is opened, and after a while they all taste like hay. A good thing to do is to date your packaged herbs when you buy them, and throw them out at least twice a year. Anyhow, back to orégano, try tucking it into a roast leg of lamb sometime; it's delicious.

## LAMB OREGANO *(Riganato)*

2½ pounds boned leg of lamb
1 or 2 cloves garlic
5 tablespoons butter or other fat
1 cup hot water
2 tablespoons lemon juice
1 teaspoon orégano

12  *small new potatoes, peeled and whole*
*Salt and pepper to taste*
*More water if needed*

Cut the boned lamb into 10 pieces of about equal size. Peel garlic and cut into slivers lengthwise to get 10 slivers. Cut a slit in each piece of lamb and insert a sliver of garlic. Heat butter in stewpot over moderate heat and brown lamb on all sides. Pour off grease and reserve. Add wateɪ and lemon juice, cover and reduce heat to a simmer for 1 hour. Add orégano and simmer another 30 minutes. Pour off contents of pot and reserve. Dry out stewpot, return grease (adding more if needed), raise heat to moderate high and brown the potatoes. Return lamb and liquid to pot, adding more water if needed. Season to taste, reduce heat and simmer 30 minutes. *Serves 6.*

THE TURKS like lamb and eggplant together, too, although the combination is handled a little differently in this recipe than in the Greek version. Here the eggplant is used as a serving bed, much as one might use mashed potatoes or noodles. What makes this dish really interesting, however, is the use of pine nuts, which make nice, crunchy surprises throughout the stew. If you can't get pine nuts (and they are difficult to store successfully), you may use slivered almonds, but the pine nuts are sweeter and their flavor blends better.

## TURKISH LAMB STEW

1  *good-size eggplant*
3  *tablespoons flour*
1  *teaspoon seasoned salt*
2  *pounds boned lamb, cubed*
3  *tablespoons butter*
1  *onion, thinly sliced*

1 No. 2 can tomatoes
½ cup sake or dry white wine
½ cup water
¼ cup pine nuts
2 tablespoons butter
Salt and pepper to taste

Put eggplant, whole and unpeeled, in a 350° oven and bake until quite soft. While it is baking, put flour and salt in paper bag and shake cubes of lamb to coat thoroughly. Put butter in stewpot over medium heat and brown the pieces of lamb lightly. Add onion and continue to sauté until yellow but not brown. Add tomatoes, sake and water. Cover and simmer 40 minutes, or until lamb is quite tender. Add pine nuts and cook another 5 minutes. The eggplant should be well baked by this time. Peel it and mash it thoroughly in a saucepan over low heat, adding butter and salt and pepper to taste. Serve mashed eggplant on individual plates and spoon lamb stew on top of it. *Serves 4.*

OLIVES ought to be used in cooking more often than they are, in my opinion. They are nice surprises to find in your food and they do not affect the taste of the dish so strongly that one hesitates to use them. True, they are relatively expensive, but a little bitty jar of green or ripe olives can transform a stew from something mundane into a happening. The following recipe from Morocco gets some of its oompf from olives. Of course, there's ginger and parsley to affect the final taste, too. And, by the way, if chopping parsley bugs you, try using the kitchen scissors on it.

### CHICKEN MOROCCO
### (Braised Chicken with Olives)

½ cup flour

½ teaspoon salt
1 frying chicken, 3½ pounds, disjointed
3 tablespoons butter
1½ cups chicken broth
2 medium onions, sliced
½ teaspoon ground ginger
Several shakes paprika
¼ teaspoon freshly ground black pepper
4 tablespoons chopped parsley
1 7-ounce jar pitted green olives
¼ cup water
2 tablespoons lemon juice
Instant flour

Put ½ cup flour and salt in paper bag and shake chicken pieces in it. Melt butter in stewpot over moderate heat, and brown chicken lightly. Add broth, onions, ginger, paprika, pepper and parsley. Cover and reduce heat to slow simmer for 45 minutes. Near end of cooking time, drain olives into small saucepan, add water and bring to brisk boil for 3 minutes. Pour off water and add olives to pot, stirring in and simmering for a couple of minutes. Remove chicken and olives from pot with slotted spoon to serving dish and remove pot from heat. Pour lemon juice over the chicken, and if sauce is too thin, thicken with instant flour to desired consistency. Pour sauce over chicken and serve. *Serves 6.*

Couscous (pronounced "koos-koos") is made of durum wheat and is very similar to tiny pellets of macaroni or finely chopped raw spaghetti. It is steamed, rather than boiled, and makes a delicious serving bed for chicken or lamb stew. Its origin is North Africa, where it is also used with fruit as a dessert. You would probably have to go to a specialty store to buy it, but it is worth the search if you are looking for something unusual. The following couscous is made with chicken and uses saffron; it is different and delightful.

## COUSCOUS

*1 frying chicken, 3½ pounds, disjointed*
*5 onions, sliced*
*5 cups chicken broth*
*1 cup chopped parsley*
*1 tablespoon dried chervil*
*3 teaspoons salt*
*2 pinches saffron*
*2 teaspoons fresh grated ginger, or 4 teaspoons ground ginger*
*1 teaspoon white pepper*
*1 pound couscous*
*½ pound butter*

Put chicken, onions, broth, parsley, chervil, salt, saffron, ginger and white pepper in the stewpot. Cover and bring to a good simmer for 45 minutes. After chicken has cooked for 25 minutes, drain off 4 cups of broth and melt butter in it. Pour this over the couscous in a 3-quart saucepan, stir thoroughly and set over the very lowest heat with a lid. Let sit 20 minutes (while chicken finishes cooking). Then put couscous in the bottom of your largest serving dish and pour contents of pot over it. Let sit 5 minutes before you serve. *Serves 6.*

IN CERTAIN PARTS of Africa, peanuts are frequently used in cooking; they are pounded into a smooth paste with a mallet. But you don't have to spend half a day pounding peanuts; you can use the peanuts that some hard-working manufacturer has already pounded, namely, peanut butter. Actually, to get the full flavor of the peanut, you should pound it yourself, as that afore-mentioned hard-working manufacturer omits the flavor-packed kernel from the peanut in order to obtain a product that does not go stale or rancid over a great length of time. If you want to make your own peanut butter, you can do so in the blender. Put a large handful of husked peanuts into the blender with about 1 tablespoonful oil and turn on the machine. It takes some time to get fully pulverized peanuts and is very noisy, so do it on a day when your nerves are in good shape.

## AFRICAN PEANUT STEW

1 *frying chicken, 3½ pounds, disjointed*
1 *cup flour*
4 *tablespoons butter*
1 *large onion, sliced*
½ *cup peanut butter*
1½ *cups hot water*
2 *teaspoons ground ginger, or 1 teaspoon fresh grated ginger*
1 *teaspoon seasoned salt*
¼ *teaspoon black pepper*
2 *green peppers, seeded and chopped*
½ *package frozen sliced green beans*
1 *No. 2 can tomatoes*

Dredge chicken in flour to coat well. Melt butter in stewpot over medium heat, and brown the chicken pieces. Add onion and cook until tender. Add more flour if needed to take up excess grease. Mix peanut butter and hot water until smoothly blended, and add to chicken and onions. Add ginger, seasoned salt and pepper. Cover and simmer 40 minutes. Add green pepper, green beans and tomatoes, and simmer another 10 minutes. *Serves 6.*

A GOOD MANY years ago I worked for the Consulate General of Pakistan, and we had on our staff, curiously enough, a full-blooded Iroquois Indian as well as a youthful Iranian. These two gentlemen took an immediate dislike to each other, and one day at a reception, the Iranian approached the Indian with the query: "So you're an Indian? Where's your wigwam?" To which the Indian countered so swiftly that one suspected him of rehearsing it: "So you're a Persian? Where's your flying carpet?"

One can easily imagine oneself aboard a flying carpet bound for some exotic corner of the world while eating the stew which follows. It is enlivened by celery, cinnamon and nutmeg, and is a real taste treat.

## IRANIAN BEEF STEW

2  *tablespoons butter*
1  *large onion, thinly sliced*
2  *pounds lean round steak, cubed*
1  *teaspoon salt*
½  *teaspoon freshly ground pepper*
1  *teaspoon cinnamon*
½  *teaspoon nutmeg*
1  *cup beef bouillon*
2  *tablespoons butter*
1  *cup chopped parsley*
4  *cups diced celery*
3  *tablespoons lemon juice*

Melt butter in stewpot and sauté onion until very lightly browned. Remove onion and reserve. Add meat, salt, pepper, cinnamon and nutmeg to hot butter in pot, lower heat and stir while meat browns lightly. Return onions to pot and add bouillon. Cover and simmer about 1½ hours, or until beef is tender. Empty pot and wipe dry with a paper towel, put it back over medium heat, melt 2 tablespoons butter and sauté parsley and celery 15 minutes. Add lemon juice and return beef stew to pot to simmer 10 minutes before serving. *Serves 6.*

AND NOW we come to that part of the world to which we are indebted for the noble curry. The extra-special curry which I learned to make when I was working for the government of Pakistan is to be found in the chapter called "Special Stews for Guests." But here are two other curries for you to experiment with. As with chili powder in chili, curry powder must be ladled out in accordance with the taste of the eater—I like a good hot curry, but not everybody agrees with me. There are tremendous differences in the relative strengths of the curries available in the market, so you must taste your curry as you add the powder until you have the desired flavor.

## CHICKEN CURRY

3  *tablespoons flour*
1  *teaspoon turmeric*
½  *teaspoon seasoned salt*
5  *tablespoons butter*
1  *roasting chicken, 4 to 5 pounds, disjointed*
1  *large onion, sliced*
2  *cloves garlic, pressed*
2  *tablespoons (more or less) curry powder*
2  *teaspoons coriander*
4  *whole cloves*
2  *sticks cinnamon*
1  *cup chicken broth*
Beurre manié, *if required*

Put flour, turmeric and seasoned salt in paper bag and shake well. Melt butter in stewpot over moderate heat. Shake pieces of chicken in flour mixture and brown well in butter. Remove chicken. Put onion, garlic, curry powder, coriander, cloves and cinnamon sticks into pot and sauté, stirring frequently, until onion is yellow. Add browned chicken and broth to pot, cover and simmer slowly 1 hour, adding more broth if needed. When chicken is cooked, remove from pot and thicken sauce, if desired, with *beurre manié* made with 1 tablespoon flour blended into 1 tablespoon butter. *Serves 6.*

As YOU MAY KNOW, curry powder does not mean powdered curry; there is no such thing. Curry powder is a blend of powdered spices and it varies with the person doing the blending, which accounts for the considerable differences among commercially prepared curry powders, with the kind packaged by U.S. spice makers distinctly on the bland side. The following recipe lets you make your own curry powder, and it has considerably more authority than the pre-packaged kind. Proceed with caution, and be prepared to exercise your taste buds.

## FISH CURRY

3  *tablespoons butter*
1  *teaspoon crushed red pepper*
½  *teaspoon turmeric*
½  *teaspoon salt*
2  *pounds halibut steak, cubed*
1  *large onion, sliced*
3  *cloves garlic, whole*
½  *teaspoon turmeric*
½  *teaspoon ground coriander*
½  *teaspoon ground cumin*
½  *teaspoon ground cardamom*
½  *teaspoon ground cinnamon*
1  *teaspoon salt*
1  *large onion, finely grated*

3 *medium tomatoes, peeled and sliced*
1 *cup yoghurt*

Heat butter in stewpan over medium heat. Mix red pepper, ½ teaspoon turmeric and ½ teaspoon salt in paper bag and shake cubes of fish to thoroughly coat. Brown the fish in hot butter and remove from pot. Put sliced onion and whole garlic in pot (adding butter if needed), and sauté gently until brown. Mix ½ teaspoon turmeric, coriander, cumin, cardamom, cinnamon and 1 teaspoon salt with grated onion and add to stewpot. Add tomatoes. Simmer gently for 12 minutes. Beat yoghurt and add slowly to pot, mixing in well, and let cook 5 minutes. Add cubes of fried fish and simmer an additional 10 minutes. Remove cloves of garlic and serve. *Serves 6.*

FROM INDIA to China the road is rough and rugged, both geographically and ideologically, but from curry powder to ginger is only a step or two in a cookbook. Fortunately, fresh ginger root is readily available in many parts of this country, including the one in which I live, and if you can get it, by all means use it wherever ginger is called for, except, possibly, in gingerbread. Fresh ginger may be kept for months in the refrigerator without losing its pizzazz, and may be minced or grated for most cooking purposes. Substitute fresh for powdered ginger on a one-for-two ratio, i.e., one teaspoon minced or grated ginger for two teaspoons powdered.

Most recipes for Chinese cooking seem to be designed for huge families or for restaurants and are difficult to duplicate at home. The reason for this is that most Chinese dishes call for a tablespoon of this and a teaspoon of that, and by "this" and "that," they mean chopped shrimp or bamboo shoots or other items which are normally purchased in much larger quantities. Unless one is going to feature Chinese cuisine for two or three weeks, it simply does not make sense to acquire the large variety of items required for chop suey, for example. I have, however, one Chinese recipe —and it's a stew to boot!—that does not require arduous shopping and that is easy to prepare on any Sunday afternoon, and here it is:

## CHINESE POT ROAST CHICKEN

1  teaspoon fresh ginger, finely minced
1  clove garlic, pressed
2  tablespoons sherry
2  tablespoons soy sauce
1  fryer, 3½ pounds, disjointed
10  dried Chinese mushrooms
Chicken neck, gizzard and heart
1  cup water
Chicken liver
3  tablespoons cooking oil
8  scallions, sliced
Chicken broth, as needed
1  teaspoon salt
¼  teaspoon white pepper
½  teaspoon sugar
2  tablespoons cornstarch

In a large bowl, mix ginger, garlic, sherry and soy sauce for a marinade. Marinate pieces of chicken in this for at least 30 minutes. Soak mushrooms separately in water at the same time. Put chicken neck, gizzard and heart in saucepan with cup of water, and simmer 30 minutes. While this is cooking, scald the chicken liver in a little boiling water 5 minutes, dice and set aside. Remove neck, gizzard and heart and save liquid, adding more broth if needed to make a full cup. Discard neck, and dice gizzard and heart. Put cooking oil in stewpot over medium heat and brown the marinated chicken well. Remove chicken, and add scallions, mushrooms (sliced after soaking) and the diced liver, gizzard and heart. Sauté gently for 5 minutes. Add cup of broth and marinade, and salt, pepper and sugar. Return browned chicken to pot and simmer very gently 45 minutes. Remove chicken to warm platter. Mix cornstarch very slowly with a little water to make a thin paste, and stir in pot until sauce is thickened. Pour over chicken and serve *Serves 4.*

FROM CHINA to the Philippines is but a hop, skip and jump on the map, but soy sauce, ginger and dried mushrooms get lost en route. Here is a Philippine recipe for marinated chicken and pork that will set your taste buds to tingling.

## PHILIPPINE MARINATED CHICKEN AND PORK

½ cup wine vinegar
2 teaspoons salt
½ teaspoon pepper
4 cloves garlic, sliced
1 bay leaf
1 frying chicken, 3½ pounds, disjointed
1½ pounds boned lean pork
2 tablespoons cooking oil
½ cup sake or dry white wine
1 cup chicken broth
2 tablespoons flour

Mix vinegar, salt, pepper, garlic and bay leaf in a large bowl. Add chicken and pork and marinate at least 30 minutes. Remove meat and dry on paper towel. Put oil in stewpot over medium heat, and when hot add chicken and pork and sauté until meat is brown on all sides, adding more oil as needed. Add sake and broth, cover and simmer 45 minutes. Remove chicken and pork and keep warm. Place liquid in freezer compartment of refrigerator until fat is congealed on top (about 1 hour). Remove fat and reserve. Pour off broth and reserve. Melt 2 tablespoons reserved fat in stewpot. Stir in flour until thick paste is formed. Add reserved broth gradually, stirring constantly. Add chicken and pork and bring to boil. Reduce to simmer and heat for 10 minutes. Rice is good with this. *Serves 6.*

FROM THE PHILIPPINES we will come back to the Western world in two large hops—one to Russia and thence to Ireland, from where you ought to be able to get home by yourself. Boeuf à la Stroganoff gets its name from a nineteenth-century Russian count of the same name, who must have been quite a gourmet. The following recipe was obtained from a friend who maintains it is more authentic than most because of the red color, which it derives from tomato. Whether it is authentic or not, I can't say, but it certainly is attractive! A word of caution: Although stews are generally considered to be budget-stretchers, don't try to stretch your budget on this one. It requires the finest grade of beef you can buy, preferably filet mignon, for the meat cooks but a short time and should be tender enough to cut with a fork. So, economize on something else when you serve this dish.

## BOEUF A LA STROGANOFF

3   tablespoons butter
3   large onions, thinly sliced
1   pound mushrooms, sliced
1   can condensed tomato soup
½   cup milk
1   tablespoon Worcestershire sauce
2   shakes Tabasco sauce
2   tablespoons butter

132

2½ pounds beef tenderloin, cut in strips ½ inch
   wide
1 cup sour cream

Melt butter in stewpot over moderate heat, add onions
and sauté until just transparent. Add mushrooms and
continue sautéing another 10 minutes. Add tomato
soup and milk, and simmer another 15 minutes. Stir in
Worcestershire and Tabasco sauces and turn off heat.
Have 2 tablespoons butter hot in a large, heavy frying
pan, and sauté strips of beef quickly (not more than 5
minutes). Now stir the sour cream into the sauce, add
beef and serve. *Serves 6.*

AND NOW I will polish off this chapter with something
as familiar-sounding as your back yard, namely, Irish
stew. There are probably as many recipes for Irish stew
as there are Irishmen, and about the only ingredient on
which there is anything approaching a consensus is the
potato—but how many and what size and what *kind*
(we know one person who insists that yams are essential to an Irish stew) are variables again. Anyhow, this
particular Irish stew (which is very authentic, as it
came from the local bartender) uses rib lamb chops instead of stew meat and is very elegant indeed.

## IRISH STEW

2 tablespoons bacon drippings
12 small rib lamb chops
3 cups water
1 package dry onion soup mix
12 small new potatoes, peeled and whole
24 small white onions, peeled and whole
24 small carrots, whole
1 teaspoon mace
6 shallots, sliced

*1 large clove garlic, pressed*
*½ cup chopped chives*
*½ cup chopped celery leaves*
*Instant flour*

Melt fat in stewpot over moderately high heat, and brown chops well on both sides. Pour off excess fat. Add water and bring to boil, then add onion soup mix. Cover and reduce heat to slow simmer for 1 hour. Add potatoes, onions, carrots, mace and shallots, and continue simmering for ½ hour. Remove chops to heated platter. Add garlic, chives and celery leaves and simmer another 10 or 15 minutes, until onions are tender. Remove from heat and let sit several minutes before shaking in instant flour to thicken sauce to desired consistency. *Serves 6.*

# 5

## OFF THE BEATEN PATH

*(Variety Meat and Game Stews)*

I DON'T KNOW whether this is true throughout the country, but in California, such delectable meat products as sweetbreads and calf's liver are lumped by the butchers into a category they designate as "offal." This makes me squirm, and, furthermore, it simply isn't true. According to my dictionary, "offal" means "the parts of a butchered animal that are considered inedible by human beings." Obviously our butchers need a further education in public relations, but I believe in pampering butchers and never say anything. I give them the benefit of the doubt and assume they don't know what the word means. The term the butchers should be using is "variety meats," which refers to the internal organs, such as brains, kidney, etc., although the word "offal" is acceptable usage for these items in Great Britain.

When dealing with variety meats, special care should be taken that they are fresh, or at least fresh-frozen (many variety meats cannot be frozen successfully), as they deteriorate rapidly. They should be cooked within a short time of purchase, preferably the same day, or, if frozen, immediately after thawing. They should be carefully inspected and discolored portions removed, and, generally speaking, they should be washed before cooking.

If these precautions are taken, variety meats offer

tasty and interesting alternatives to more mundane fare. Of course, I realize that there are people who do not consider brains and sweetbreads palatable food, no matter how carefully inspected or thoroughly washed, and nothing can be done about them, for their objections are insuperable. I am reminded of a southern Italian girl who thought raw squid a great delicacy, but was sick to her stomach when told she had eaten beef tongue. If you consider variety meats indeed "offal," then this chapter is not for you.

On the other hand, for those of us who relish them, variety meats provide oodles of vitamins and minerals ordinarily not so readily or so abundantly available. Liver, for example, is, as everyone knows, an unusually rich source of iron, vitamin A and other goodies, and the other variety meats are, for the most part, similarly endowed. However, enough people are squeamish about eating organ foods that I would not recommend serving any of the variety-meat stews at a dinner party without double checking with your guests in advance.

This chapter also includes recipes for game stews for those of you who have access to such specialties as venison, rabbit or wild duck. The recipes assume that the meat comes to you ready to cook; if you need instructions for skinning, butchering or de-feathering the animal, you'll have to get another book.

SEVERAL YEARS AGO my husband and I lunched in a small restaurant in Palo Alto whose menu included Chicken Giblets in Wine Sauce. It was extremely tasty, so much so that my husband decided to try to duplicate it in our own kitchen. He was at that time encountering difficulties with the plot for a Michael Shayne book, and, whenever that happens, he becomes more active than usual in the kitchen, so we ate variations on the chicken-giblet theme for weeks. I believe he lay awake nights thinking about giblets instead of about Shayne, but he tells me that cooking helps his mind work out the devious designs he needs for his writing. At any rate, at the end of about a month, he had produced the following recipe for chicken giblet stew *and* a satisfactory Shayne plot. I have forgotten the name of the book, but the stew is superb, as you will discover when you try it yourself.

## CHICKEN GIBLET STEW, SHANTY SHAYNE

1  pound chicken livers (halved)
3  tablespoons flour
1  teaspoon seasoned salt
8  tablespoons butter
1½ pounds chicken gizzards (halved)
1½  cans chicken broth
½  cup sake or dry white wine
18  small pearl onions

Shake halved livers in a paper bag containing the flour and seasoned salt. Melt butter in stewpot over moderately high heat, and quickly brown the pieces of liver on both sides. Remove from pot and set aside. Shake halved gizzards in the seasoned flour and reduce heat under pot to medium. Brown gizzards thoroughly on both sides, allowing them to cook much longer than the livers. There should be some butter left after cooking; absorb this with seasoned flour. Add chicken broth and sake, blending well with the flour, cover tightly and simmer for 1½ hours. The gizzards should be just tender enough to be chewy, but not completely cooked. Add pearl onions, peeled and whole (A note here: Don't hesitate to use tiny onions because they are difficult to peel. They aren't. Drop them into a pan of fast-boiling water, clap on a lid and boil 10 seconds. Run cold water over them at once, then cut off the root and squeeze. They will pop out of their skins with no fuss and no tears.) Continue to simmer with gizzards ½ hour or more, until onions are tender but still firm. Drop in the browned livers at the end and simmer all together not more than 5 minutes. If you wish the sauce a little thicker, remove from fire and let stand a few minutes before shaking in instant flour to desired consistency. These are truly wonderful served over egg noodles or slices of toast. *Serves 6.*

I AM MORE FOND of sweetbreads than of the other variety meats (except liver), perhaps because the name does not conjure up any revolting pictures of what I am about to eat. Sweetbreads consist of the pancreas and sometimes the thymus glands of the animal, both of which seem innocuous and edible. They have a delicate flavor and a nice firm texture, and lend themselves to a variety of cooking methods. As is the case with most organ meats, overcooking will toughen them. Calf sweetbreads are preferable to beef, because they are easier to prepare, and I have had good luck with the frozen kind.

## GLAZED SWEETBREADS

2  *pairs calf sweetbreads, fresh or frozen*
1  *heaping tablespoon flour*
½  *teaspoon salt*
¼  *teaspoon white pepper*
6  *tablespoons sweet butter*
2  *ounces cognac*
1½  *teaspoons meat glaze*
1  *teaspoon tomato paste*
3  *teaspoons (more or less) potato flour*
1½  *can chicken broth*
½  *cup sake or dry white wine*
1  *tablespoon currant jelly*

To prepare sweetbreads before cooking, simmer in

salted water 15 minutes, pour off water at once and add very cold water. When cooled, remove all skin and tough membrane. Put flour, salt and pepper in paper bag and shake sweetbreads to coat them. Lay out on a board and press flat with a spatula. Melt butter in stewpot over high heat and drop sweetbreads in, a pair at a time, pressing with spatula to flatten while they brown on both sides. Remove sweetbreads and turn out fire under pot. Add cognac, meat glaze, tomato paste and potato flour, blending into a smooth paste. Stir in chicken broth, sake and jelly, and turn heat to medium, stirring constantly until smooth. Return browned sweetbreads to sauce, turning to cover and coat them with sauce, and simmer very gently for 40 minutes, stirring occasionally. *Serves 4.*

WHEN WE first started eating sweetbreads at our house, none of the cookbooks we had at the time contained a recipe for cooking them. So we made one up. I guess we were on a curry binge then, because that's what we did, and curried sweetbreads have been a staple item on the menu ever since. Try them cooked this way; they are delicious, for the curry is a mild one, so as not to completely overpower the sweetbreads.

## CURRIED SWEETBREADS

2  *pairs calf sweetbreads, fresh or frozen*
1½  *cups white wine*
4  *tablespoons sweet butter*
1  *large onion, finely chopped*
½  *pound fresh mushrooms, thinly sliced*
2  *cloves garlic, pressed*
2  *medium apples, peeled, cored and sliced*
2  *medium tomatoes, peeled and sliced*
1  *teaspoon ground ginger*
1½  *tablespoons curry powder*

1 tablespoon sugar
½ cup beef bouillon
Salt and pepper to taste
Instant flour

Prepare sweetbreads as in Glazed Sweetbreads recipe, and break into segments. Marinate in white wine for 1 hour. Near the end of this hour, melt butter in stewpot over low heat and gently sauté onions and mushrooms together until onions are transparent. Add garlic, apples, tomatoes, ginger, curry powder and sugar. Add bouillon, and salt and pepper to taste, and simmer several minutes. Remove from heat and let cool a few minutes before shaking in instant flour to thicken well. Add sweetbreads with the marinade and simmer 35 minutes. *Serves 6.*

BRAINS are often substituted for sweetbreads and are very good cooked with scrambled eggs. To prepare brains, they should be soaked for about 3 hours in cold water to which a tablespoon of vinegar or lemon juice has been added. Then they must be skinned and soaked again to remove all traces of blood. As with sweetbreads, they should be blanched by simmering gently in water to cover (again with vinegar or lemon juice) for 20 minutes for calf brains, 25 minutes for others.

## BRAIN RAGOUT

1 pound calf brains
1 package frozen asparagus tips
½ cup butter
½ pound mushrooms, sliced
6 tablespoons flour
2 cups light cream
1 cup chicken broth
2 egg yolks

140

1 teaspoon salt
¼ teaspoon white pepper
½ teaspoon paprika
Dash nutmeg
1 tablespoon dry sherry
1 tablespoon Worcestershire sauce

Prepare brains as above and set aside. Defrost asparagus tips and set aside. Melt butter in stewpot and sauté mushrooms 5 minutes. Blend in the flour, then the cream and chicken broth. Add brains and simmer gently for a few minutes while you pour off ½ cup of the sauce into a small pan and beat the egg yolks into it. Turn out heat under pot and add the egg mixture to pot, then turn in asparagus tips and stir gently for a few minutes over very low heat while you add salt, white pepper, paprika, nutmeg, sherry and Worcestershire sauce. Serve at once. *Serves 4.*

ONE OF the big advantages of the variety meats is their lack of waste; there is no bone or fat to be paid for but never eaten, nor do they shrink during the cooking process. Kidneys are good examples of this, and, furthermore, they make excellent stews. To prepare kidneys, wash them in cold water and remove the outer skin, then soak them in cold, salted water for 2 or 3 hours. When ready to cook them, remove the white centers and tubes with a pair of manicure scissors or a sharp, pointed knife. When purchasing kidneys, veal or lamb are preferable, but beef, mutton and pork are also good, especially in stews, as they profit from the longer cooking time.

## LAMB OR VEAL KIDNEY STEW

1½ pounds lamb or veal kidneys
6 tablespoons butter

1 bunch scallions, thinly sliced with stems
1 pound mushrooms, sliced
1 small green pepper, diced
1 tablespoon chopped parsley
Salt and pepper to taste
½ teaspoon paprika
½ cup sake or dry white wine
3 ounces light rum
½ cup sour cream

Prepare the kidneys as above and cut into thin slices. Melt butter in stewpot over moderate heat, and sauté scallions, mushrooms and green pepper together for 5 minutes. Add sliced kidneys and chopped parsley, and season to taste with salt and pepper and paprika. Add sake and light rum, cover tightly and simmer for 1½ hours. Just before serving, stir in sour cream. *Serves 4.*

IF YOU screw up your face at the thought of eating kidney, it may be because you have had the unfortunate experience of eating beef kidney that has not been carefully trimmed or properly cooked. Beef kidney can have a strong taste, but it comes from the fat rather than the meat. Beef kidney should always be blanched. The following is a method of cooking beef kidney which is especially designed for people who think they don't like it. If you belong to this category, try this recipe and you'll change your mind.

## BEEF KIDNEY STEW

2 small beef kidneys
1 tablespoon vinegar
2 tablespoons butter
2 tablespoons flour
1 cup beef bouillon
2 tablespoons tomato paste
Salt and pepper to taste

142

The kidneys should be prepared well ahead of cooking time so they may be chilled in the refrigerator before attempting to slice them very thinly. Soak for at least 2 hours in salted water, then remove all fat and white membranes. Blanch for 20 minutes in water with 1 tablespoon vinegar, then chill for 1 hour before slicing. Melt butter in stewpot and sauté sliced kidneys until lightly browned. Remove from pot, stir in flour and then beef bouillon and tomato paste. Return kidneys to pot and season with salt and pepper to taste. Simmer very, very slowly for 20 minutes. *Serves 4.*

THE FOLLOWING recipe calls for pork kidney, but any of the other types of kidney could be used with equally tasty results. Veal and lamb kidney do not require blanching, as they are tenderer and more delicately flavored than the other varieties. This is a hearty dish that needs no accompaniment other than a loaf of bread and a jug of wine—and a hungry group of people.

## PORK KIDNEY STEW

2  *to 3 pounds pork kidneys, sliced*
4  *cups beef bouillon*
1  *large onion, chopped*
3  *stalks celery with leaves, sliced*
3  *large carrots, diced*
3  *medium potatoes, quartered*
*Salt and pepper to taste*
4  *slices bacon, diced*
2  *tablespoons flour*

Blanch the kidneys as for Beef Kidney Stew recipe. Put bouillon, sliced kidneys, onion and celery all in stewpot and bring to a boil. Cover, reduce heat and simmer for 2½ hours. Add carrots, potatoes and salt and pepper to taste and continue cooking until carrots are tender, about 40 minutes. Just before serving, brown the diced bacon in a heavy frying pan, and blend in flour. Add this to the stew and simmer another 10 minutes before serving. *Serves 6.*

No DISCUSSION of variety meats would be complete without instructions for making the stew given below. It is, I believe, indigenous to the Western United States, and comes from the days when there were really and truly cowboys and roundups and cattle drives and all the rest of it. When a beef animal was slaughtered, all of its innards were tossed into a pot for the stew of the evening (ragout de maison, perhaps), which was called, in the colorful language of that era and group: son-of-a-bitch stew.

My husband's recollection of the original recipe, retained from a boyhood spent on the Pecos River in West Texas, is that the roundup cook simply removed the marrow gut, heart, kidneys, liver, sweetbreads, tongue and brains from a freshly butchered yearling. He started the stew by tossing the cut-up marrow gut into his biggest hot pot and frying it out well before adding water to boil and then tossing in all the other goodies with whatever vegetables he had on hand. This agglomeration was cooked until the meat was tender enough to chew.

Since none of us butchers yearlings these days, and I know of no market that sells marrow gut, we have worked out the following compromise, which we still call:

## SON-OF-A-BITCH STEW

  4  *pounds marrow bones, split*
  1  *pound beef heart, cubed*
  1½  *pounds beef kidney, blanched and cubed*

2  medium onions, sliced
2  stalks celery, sliced
Water to cover
½  pound beef liver, cubed
Salt and pepper to taste
1  can whole kernel corn
1  package frozen okra

Remove marrow from the split bones and toss into the stewpot over low heat. Allow to cook slowly for 20 minutes before adding the heart and kidneys and the onions and celery. Continue cooking over low heat, stirring and turning frequently for another 20 minutes. Add water, cover tightly and simmer very gently for 2 hours or more, until meat is tender. Add liver, and salt and pepper to taste. Simmer 15 minutes before adding corn and okra. Cook another 10 minutes before serving. *Serves 8.*

MY HUSBAND AND I are not hunters, so we are unfamiliar with the fine points of shooting, skinning and or dismembering deer, duck and other wild creatures who fall victim to man's superior weaponry. I prefer to admire a deer bounding gracefully through the woods without considering how to go about killing it, and when the cat brings in a rabbit or a squirrel she gets no felicitations from me. When I identify the various kinds of wild fowl at the local bird refuge, I do so with all the objectivity of a vegetarian. On the other hand, I enjoy eating meat, including game, and do so without any qualms of conscience. If I am given a haunch of venison or saddle of hare, I simply close my mind to any thoughts about their sources and am quite comfortable. I suspect I am not alone in this ambiguous attitude; it is one of those compromises we make in order to preserve our sanity.

Unfortunately, if one is to have a really good game

dish, one must consider the circumstances in which the animal was killed. If it was frightened or angry, the meat will be tougher and stronger in flavor ("gamy") than if the animal was unaware of its impending doom. One does not like to make too many inquiries in this direction, however, so it is better to play safe and marinate, particularly the flesh from larger animals, such as deer. Age is an important factor, too, and, as this is also usually difficult to determine, cooking times vary considerably, but all game should be cooked until well done.

Wine, or wine vinegar and water, is the customary marinade, but beer or buttermilk can also be used and results in a slightly mellower flavor; marinating time is overnight.

## VENISON STEW

4 pounds venison, cubed and marinated overnight as above
4 tablespoons flour
2 teaspoons seasoned salt
6 tablespoons butter
2 cups dry red wine
2 cups beef bouillon
½ cup sake or dry white wine
6 carrots, sliced
6 stalks celery with leaves, diced
2 medium onions, sliced
2 cloves garlic, pressed
2 bay leaves
2 tablespoons chopped parsley
½ teaspoon fines herbes (chives, chervil and thyme)
Salt and pepper to taste
1 pound mushrooms, sliced
1 cup sour cream
2 teaspoons paprika

Remove venison from marinade and dry between paper towels. Put flour and seasoned salt in paper bag and shake the pieces of venison in it to coat well. Melt butter in stewpot over moderate heat and brown the venison well on all sides. Add wine, bouillon and sake, and bring to light boil. Add carrots, celery, onions, garlic, bay leaves, parsley and fines herbes. Add salt and pepper to taste. Cover and simmer 1 hour, or until meat is fairly tender. Add mushrooms and simmer 20 minutes. Stir in sour cream and paprika and serve immediately. *Serves 8.*

AMONG OUR ACQUAINTANCES in Southern California is a young man who literally "lives off the land." In season, he hunts fowl, small animals, deer and javelina (wild pig); he raises his own fruit and vegetables (in fact, he calls the garden his "stew patch"); he fishes; he keeps hounds for hunting and goats for milk, and, in this way, feeds not only himself but his wife and two children as well. We who rely upon civilization's complex system of making food available to us can only stand in awe of such resourcefulness. Not too surprisingly, he also cooks, and his roast pig is a marvel of succulence and flavor. It is to him (he is also a writer) to whom I am indebted for the following recipe.

## VENISON CHILI

4 *pounds venison, cubed and marinated overnight*
½ *cup vegetable oil*
1½ *pounds summer or Italian squash, cubed*
3 *green peppers, seeded and sliced*
1 *large onion, chopped*
1 *tablespoon chili powder*
1 *teaspoon salt*
3 *chicken bouillon cubes*
3 *teaspoons ketchup*

2 tablespoons wine vinegar
2 teaspoons brown sugar
1 teaspoon fines herbes (chives, chervil, thyme and parsley)
3 whole tomatoes
10 small corn tortillas, cut in 1-inch squares
¾ pound grated longhorn cheese

Remove venison from marinade and dry between paper towels. Heat oil in stewpot and throw in cubed venison and squash together. Stir frequently as it cooks for 10 minutes. Add green pepper, onion and chili powder, and continue stirring while you add salt, chicken bouillon cubes, ketchup, vinegar, brown sugar and fines herbes. Continue cooking until squash is tender, then add whole tomatoes and tortillas. Cook until the skins slip off the tomatoes. Discard skins. Shake grated cheese over the top and cover long enough to melt cheese. Remove pot from heat and let sit at least 15 minutes before serving. *Serves 8.*

RABBIT is frequently available in butcher shops and supermarkets, but that is tame rabbit and not properly the subject of this chapter. To stew tame rabbit, use any of the recipes for chicken (Chapter 2). Wild rabbit has a stronger flavor and is more of an acquired taste. You can marinate or not, as you wish, in a mixture of half water, half wine, with a few peppercorns and a bay leaf tossed in for good measure.

## WILD RABBIT STEW

½ pound salt pork, diced
½ medium onion, thinly sliced
1 cup sliced mushrooms
1 rabbit, cut into cooking pieces
1½ tablespoons flour

½   teaspoon seasoned salt
2   ounces brandy or light rum, warmed
1   cup chicken broth
½   cup sake
½   lemon rind, chopped
10   peppercorns
1   stalk celery with leaves, chopped
Instant flour, if desired

Put diced salt pork in stewpot over moderate heat until well browned. Remove with slotted spoon and reserve. Sauté onion and mushrooms 10 minutes in fat. Remove and reserve. Now sauté pieces of rabbit shaken in flour and seasoned salt, until lightly browned. Pour brandy or rum over the pieces and set afire. Shake pot until flames go out. Add chicken broth and sake. Tie up lemon rind, peppercorns and celery in a cloth bag and add to pot with bits of browned salt pork. Cover tightly and simmer for 1 hour or more, until rabbit is tender. Remove seasoning bag and return onions and mushrooms to pot. Simmer 5 minutes and remove from heat. Thicken with a little instant flour, if desired. *Serves 4.*

As in the case with rabbit, there is considerable difference in taste between the duck that has been pampered and protected on a commercial duck farm and the duck shot at dawn by some alleged sportsman concealed and shivering behind a duck blind and playing nasty little tricks on his quarry like setting out decoys. If you have never tasted wild duck, you may find it a little unpleasant at first, but stick with it and you will soon come to relish it as a special taste treat. And whether you are a novice or an old hand, you will find the following wild duck stew exciting and delectable.

149

# WILD DUCK STEW WITH WINE

*Salt and pepper*
*2 wild ducks, disjointed*
*1 cup red burgundy wine*
*½ cup brandy*
*1½ tablespoons chopped parsley*
*2 medium onions, sliced*
*1 teaspoon fines herbs (chives, chervil and thyme)*
*¼ teaspoon nutmeg*
*1 bay leaf*
*¼ pound butter*
*1 clove garlic, pressed*
*½ pound sliced mushrooms*
*Instant flour*

Shake salt and pepper over the ducks and put the pieces in a large glass bowl or enamel pot. Add wine, brandy, parsley, onions, fines herbes, nutmeg and bay leaf. Let marinate for 6 hours, stirring occasionally. Remove duck and dry between paper towels. Strain marinade and reserve. Melt butter in stewpot over moderate heat and brown duck on both sides, adding garlic near the end. Add strained marinade and mushrooms, cover tightly and simmer 1½ to 2 hours, until duck is tender. Remove from heat and let sit 5 minutes before shaking in instant flour to thicken sauce to desired consistency. Return to heat and bring to boil before serving. *Serves 4.*

As WILD DUCKS are considerably more active than their tame and sedentary cousins, they do not accumulate very much fat and hence can be dry. The following recipe avoids this possibility by ladling on the butter, which, with cream and thyme, yields a very luscious dish indeed.

# WILD DUCK STEW WITH BUTTER AND CREAM

2  *wild ducks, disjointed*
*Water to cover*
3  *stalks celery, sliced*
1  *large onion, thinly sliced*
8  *tablespoons butter*
½  *cup cream*
1  *teaspoon thyme*

Put ducks in stewpot with a little water, barely enough to cover. Stew, uncovered, for 30 minutes or until almost all water is evaporated. Add celery, onion and butter, and continue cooking with cover off until juices are absorbed and duck is browned. Add cream and thyme, cover and simmer 20 minutes. *Serves 4.*

# 6

## SAVING PENNIES

### (Economy Stews)

ONE TENDS to think of "economy" and "stew" in the same breath, as if there were no other reason for making a stew than to save money. In a way, this is true, as a stew, even when made with relatively costly ingredients, usually makes a good many servings and/or feeds the family for days. When my husband was serving his apprenticeship as a writer and was living alone, he would make a stew on Monday and eat it on Tuesday, Wednesday, Thursday, Friday, Saturday and Sunday. In this way, he had tasty, nourishing food on a modest budget, and only had to cook once a week. In many parts of the world, the stewpot is kept going on the back of the stove all of the time, and bits of meat, bones and vegetables are added as they become available. This kind of stew literally costs nothing and is made without visible effort.

Readers of this cookbook will know by now that this cook/writer does not hold with the view that economy is a stew's primary reason for being. On the contrary, it is a dividend, a bonus, a welcome side effect, or even a coincidence. If you have learned your lesson well, you make a stew because it tastes good, because it is nourishing, because it is an exciting method of cooking offering an infinitude of possibilities of ingredients and combinations thereof.

153

And, by the way, some of the best stews are also economical, which is what this chapter is about. Some of the cheaper cuts of meat are good for stewing and nothing else. Oxtails, for example. And lamb riblets. And pigs' feet. They all need the long, slow, moist cooking that is stewing, and would not be edible cooked in any other way. These cuts of meat are cheap because they contain a lot of bone and/or a lot of fat, both waste products, except that the bone and the fat provide richness for your stew broth that is obtainable from no other source. Unfortunately, they do not make for dainty eating and are hardly ever seen at parties.

It was originally my intention to quote an estimate of the cost of preparing each of the stews in this chapter, but I retired that idea because of the wide variations in prices in the different parts of the country, as well as seasonal price fluctuations. However, my husband and I did price out several of the stews (I got his help because I am an absolute dud at arithmetic), and, for your edification, we made the stewed chicken backs and wings for six for $1.06 (that includes the cost of the salt and pepper), and the pigs' feet and beans for $1.25.

As NOTED PREVIOUSLY, my husband is a stew-maker without equal. His idea of the ideal way to spend a day off from writing is to prepare a stew. He spends the morning selecting the ingredients and the afternoon assembling them, and the result is always superb. He takes particular pride in making a delectable dish out of a cheap cut of meat, and one of his favorites is lamb necks. As is the case with all bony portions, the meat itself is succulent and toothsome. You don't have to eat it with your fingers, but it tastes better that way.

# STEWED LAMB NECKS WITH MACARONI

3 pounds lamb necks
2 tablespoons flour
1 teaspoon seasoned salt
4 cups water
1 package dry onion soup mix
1 large onion, diced
2 tablespoons chopped parsley
3 celery stalks, sliced
1 green pepper, seeded and sliced
1 heaping teaspoon fines herbes (chives, chervil and thyme)
Water if needed
4 ounces elbow macaroni

Have your butcher cut the thick slices of lamb neck into halves. Trim all excess fat off the outside and drop into stewpot over high heat. Brown into crisp cracklings, remove from pot and reserve. Put flour and seasoned salt in paper bag, shake lamb necks in bag, then brown the pieces in hot fat on all sides. Absorb any remaining fat with seasoned flour from the bag. Add water and bring to a good boil. Shake in dry onion soup mix. Add onion, parsley, celery stalks, green pepper and fines herbes. Return cracklings to pot. Cover and simmer gently for 2 hours or more, until meat is tender but not ready to fall from bone. Add water if needed to cover, and add macaroni slowly after liquid has returned to boil. Reduce heat and cook gently another 20 minutes before serving. *Serves 4.*


FROM TIME TO TIME, we are able to get lamb riblets for 9¢ a pound, which is just about cheaper than anything, especially as each riblet has quite a lot of meat on it. I don't know whether all butchers or markets have this cut of meat available as a separate product, but if you can get it, it makes truly excellent stews. The bone is small and smooth, so that it is possible to eat the riblets with a knife and fork, if you are so inclined. Orégano, which goes so well with lamb, gives this dish a gourmet touch.

## STEWED LAMB RIBLETS

4 to 5 pounds lamb riblets
8 cups water
2 packages dry chicken noodle soup mix
¾ cup barley
2 cloves garlic, pressed
3 medium onions, diced
8 stalks celery with leaves, diced
12 medium carrots, sliced lengthwise
1 large tomato, skinned and quartered
1 teaspoon orégano
½ teaspoon nutmeg
Salt and pepper to taste

Put riblets and water in stewpot and bring to rolling boil. Shake in dry soup mix and barley. Cover and reduce heat to a simmer for 2 hours or more, until riblets are quite tender but not yet ready to slip from bone. Turn off heat and dip off grease floating on top. Add garlic, onions, celery, carrots, tomato, orégano and nutmeg. Add salt and pepper to taste. Simmer 40 minutes. *Serves 6 to 8.*

A STEW made with chuck is not necessarily in the economy class, unless the meat happens to be on sale that day. In fact, you will find chuck stews in other chapters of this cookbook that do not stress economy. Therefore, the following stew should be called "Stew for the Day the Meat Is on Sale." The flavor is so unusual that you may want to try it even on a day when the meat is not on sale.

## BARBECUE BEEF STEW

5  *tablespoons bacon drippings or vegetable oil*
2½  *pounds boneless chuck, cubed*
2  *cups water*
1  *cup garlic-flavored barbecue sauce*
6  *medium carrots, sliced*
10  *small white onions, whole*
*Salt and pepper to taste*

Put fat in stewpot over medium high heat, and brown the pieces of chuck well on all sides. Add water and barbecue sauce and simmer about 1½ hours, until meat is just tender. Add carrots and onions, and salt and pepper to taste. Simmer another 40 minutes. *Serves 6.*

THE FOLLOWING STEW is included in this chapter because it is an economical boeuf bourguignonne, made with beer instead of wine, sort of a poor man's beef burgundy. Beer is a good stewing ingredient, and there are several stews using beer in this cookbook. If you have never cooked with beer, however, let me warn you that the smell is that of a brewery going full blast with all the lids off. Your family may not like it, so you'd better send them to the movies when you cook this one. Don't worry about it, though; as with most smells, you forget about it after a while. I'm not sure why this should be so, but I suspect it's that the olfactory sense, like overloaded wiring, blows a fuse.

## ECONOMY BEEF WITH BEER

4  *tablespoons bacon drippings*
2  *pounds lean stewing beef, cubed*

6 onions, sliced
1 can beef bouillon
1 cup water
1 bay leaf
1 pinch thyme
Salt and pepper to taste
Beer, as needed

Melt bacon drippings in stewpot over moderate heat and brown the beef cubes on all sides. Add onion near the end and sauté until tender. Add bouillon, water, bay leaf, thyme, salt and pepper to taste, and simmer very slowly, uncovered, for 2 to 3 hours, until meat is very tender. Have a can of beer open and add beer to the pot as it cooks down. This will probably require a full can. *Serves 4.*

ANOTHER RECIPE to try while your butcher has that sale going on good stewing beef is the following Hungarian stew (I don't know why this isn't called a goulash, maybe the Hungarians do). You know it's Hungarian from the amount of paprika used, and you know it's good because everything in it is designed to make it so. You can substitute veal or lamb for the beef, in case that is what the butcher is featuring.

## ECONOMY HUNGARIAN STEW

2 tablespoons bacon drippings
2 large onions, sliced
2 tablespoons paprika
3 pounds lean stewing beef, cubed
1 cup water
2 tablespoons tarragon vinegar
3 tablespoons tomato paste
1 clove garlic, pressed
1 green pepper, seeded and finely chopped

158

1 teaspoon basil
1 teaspoon ground chicory
Salt and pepper to taste

Melt bacon drippings in stewpot over medium heat and sauté onions until tender. Add paprika, cubed meat, water, vinegar, tomato paste, garlic, green pepper, basil, chicory and salt and pepper to taste. Cover and turn heat very low and let simmer for about 3 hours, until meat is very tender. Skim any excess fat from surface before serving. *Serves 6 to 8.*

IT WOULD BE impossible to write a cookbook on stews without dealing with oxtails, and a good oxtail stew is something to smack one's lips over. The secret to cooking oxtails is to give them plenty of time—anywhere from 3 to 5 hours of slow simmering, depending on size. Then the meat will drop from the bone and be very luscious indeed. By the way, oxtails, in this country, don't necessarily come from oxen, but from any adult member of the bovine family. The usage of the term "oxtails" is a carry-over from the British distinction between choice cuts of meat which are called beef and less choice cuts which are ascribed to oxen.

## OXTAIL RAGOUT

2 tablespoons flour
1 teaspoon seasoned salt
2 to 3 pounds oxtails, cut into serving pieces
6 tablespoons bacon drippings
1 medium onion, chopped fine
2 celery stalks with leaves, chopped fine
2 medium carrots, chopped
1 large clove garlic, pressed
1 bay leaf, crumbled
2 tablespoons chopped parsley

1 medium can tomatoes
1 cup beef bouillon
1 cup water
1 teaspoon fines herbes (chives, chervil and thyme)
Salt and pepper to taste

Put flour and seasoned salt in paper bag and shake pieces of oxtail in it to coat well. Melt grease in stewpot over moderate heat, and brown the oxtails slightly before adding onion, celery, carrots and garlic. Cook all together over moderate heat for 12 minutes, stirring frequently. Add bay leaf, parsley, tomatoes, bouillon, water and fines herbes. Season to taste, and simmer 2 or 3 hours (or more), until succulent meat slips easily off the bones. *Serves 6.*

THE FOLLOWING STEW was literally dreamed up by my stew-making husband, who often dreams about cooking. On this occasion, he woke me up in the middle of the night in great excitement to tell me about the stew he had dreamed of making for his good friend, Rutherford Montgomery. He was particularly delighted with the combination of ingredients—chicken wings for Monty and oxtails for himself. Of course, we had to try the stew the next day, and it was so good that it has become a standby at our house.

## OXTAILS AND CHICKEN WINGS, SHANTY SHAYNE

2 pounds oxtails, cut into serving pieces
4 cups water
1 package dry chicken noodle soup mix
1 pound chicken wings
½ cup rice
12 small white onions, peeled and whole
¼ teaspoon nutmeg

¼  teaspoon thyme
¼  teaspoon marjoram

Bring oxtails and water to a rolling boil in stewpot and add chicken soup mix. Cover and simmer for 3 hours or more, until meat is tender but not ready to slip from bone. Add rice, chicken wings, onions and seasonings. Simmer another 40 minutes. *Serves 4 to 6.*

CHICKEN is the most economical meat there is today, and chicken backs are so inexpensive that it just isn't possible to go wrong. There is not much meat on a chicken back, but what there is is exceptional—the "oyster" or "fillet" of the chicken, and the tail, which many people regard as a delicacy. Thus, backs, combined with wings, which have more meat but are nevertheless inexpensive, add up to the most economical, and, at the same time, one of the tastiest, stews in this entire cookbook. We usually serve this with dumplings (see Index for recipe), but it is also good with mashed potatoes or rice.

## STEWED CHICKEN BACKS AND WINGS

3  *pounds chicken backs*
1  *pound chicken wings*
*Water to cover*
1  *package dry chicken noodle soup mix*
1  *large onion, finely chopped*
3  *stalks celery with leaves, finely chopped*
*Salt and pepper to taste*
*Instant flour, if desired*

Put chicken in stewpot with water enough to cover well. Bring to a brisk boil and shake in chicken soup mix. Add onion and celery, and salt and pepper to taste. Cover and simmer 40 minutes if you plan to add dumplings. If you wish to serve without dumplings, cook 1 hour and remove from fire and let sit 5 minutes before stirring in enough instant flour to thicken sauce to desired consistency. Return to fire and bring to boil before serving. *Serves 6.*


WITH CHICKEN as inexpensive as it is today, I could almost include the entire section devoted to chicken stews in this chapter. Suffice it, here, to give you the recipe for one of my favorite methods of cooking chicken—whole, on top of the stove, in butter or margarine. This way of cooking is one of the simplest there is, and the result is truly delicious—tender, juicy, mouth-watering . . . even the breast is succulent. One word of caution: Be sure not to pierce the chicken when turning it, as then the nice juices will run out, leaving a tired, dry chicken behind. Turn the chicken with a spoon inserted in the cavity. It's a little difficult at first, but you'll soon get the hang of it.

## STEWED WHOLE CHICKEN

1 *frying chicken*
1 *teaspoon seasoned salt*
½ *teaspoon pepper*
1 *teaspoon paprika*
¼ *teaspoon nutmeg*
1 *medium onion, quartered*
4 *tablespoons butter or margarine*

Sprinkle the chicken, inside and out, with salt, pepper, paprika and nutmeg. Insert the quartered onion in the body cavity. Melt the butter or margarine in your stewpot, and brown the chicken on all sides, turning with a spoon inserted in the cavity. Reduce heat to very low, cover the pot and cook the chicken 1 to 1¼ hours, turning every 15 or 20 minutes. *Serves 4.*

THE HAM HOCK is another economical meat which makes for delicious eating. If you can get fresh ham (pork) hocks, by all means do so, but they are not as easily found as smoked hocks. When you cook ham hocks or any other cut of ham in a liquid, the resultant broth (called "pot likker," but it is really a sort of court bouillon) is an excellent medium in which to cook certain vegetables, such as cabbage, Brussels sprouts, etc. The following recipe uses cabbage, because that's what we like, but others are equally good and offer some variety.

## HAM HOCKS AND CABBAGE

2 pounds ham hocks (fresh or cured)
Water to cover
Salt, if needed
1 medium head cabbage, quartered

Cover ham hocks with water in stewpot and bring to boil. If fresh hocks are used, add salt to taste. Do not add salt to cured hocks until they are cooked, for they most likely will need none. Simmer 1 to 2 hours (the cured hocks need a longer cooking time), until meat is tender. Add cabbage and cook another ½ hour. *Serves 4.*

NOT EVERYBODY is keen on pig's feet, pickled or otherwise, but we find them succulent eating and have them often. A favorite method of cooking them is with red beans in a variation on chili con carne con frijoles. In this case, the "carne" is the pigs' feet, but if they don't turn you on, try this recipe with fresh or smoked ham hocks.

163

# PIGS' FEET AND BEANS

*1  pound red (frijole) beans*
*Water*
*½  teaspoon soda*
*3  fresh pigs' feet, halved*
*2  tablespoons chili powder*
*2  tablespoons flour*
*Vegetable oil to moisten*

Soak beans overnight in stewpot in sufficient water to stand ½ inch above beans when you start. Add water to cover if needed when you start cooking. Add soda and pigs' feet, and simmer about 2 hours, until beans and meat are tender. Remove pigs' feet from pot and set aside. Mix chili powder and flour with enough vegetable oil to make a thick paste, and stir into pot of beans. Bring to a boil, stirring well, then return pigs' feet to pot and let simmer very slowly together for another 20 minutes. *Serves 6.*

As MENTIONED in another part of this book, Texas cooks come nearly to blows over what constitutes the true frijole bean. I, all unwittingly, got into this controversy one evening at a dinner meeting of the California Writers Club. One of my table companions turned out to be a cook as well as a writer, as is so often the case, and, when he learned that I was writing a cookbook, said, "And are you going to include Texas chili beans?" "Oh yes," I replied, "and I shall say that red beans are essential." He was furious. "Red beans! Nonsense! True Texas chili beans are made with pinto beans and pinto beans only." He insisted on giving me his recipe, and I pass it along herewith without further comment, except to say that it tastes good, regardless of whose side you're on in the bean argument. Maybe they're pinto beans in Texas and red beans in Mexico.

# TEXAS CHILI BEANS

1  pound pinto beans
Water
½  teaspoon soda
½  pound salt pork, sliced
2  medium onions, sliced
¼  cup tomato ketchup
1  tablespoon chili powder
½  teaspoon orégano
½  teaspoon Worcestershire sauce
3  shakes Tabasco sauce
½  teaspoon dry mustard
1  teaspoon sugar
Salt to taste

Soak beans overnight in stewpot with water ½ inch over the top. Add water if needed to cover when you start cooking, and stir in soda. Add salt pork and bring to a slow simmer for 1 hour. Add the onions. Mix all remaining ingredients together in a small bowl, and stir into beans, adding salt to taste after the other is well mixed. Continue cooking about 1 more hour, until beans are tender. *Serves 6.*

ONE OF the most famous ragouts in the world is made entirely of vegetables and is extremely delicious. It is named ratatouille, which is rather a mouthful, so call it "vegetable stew" and be done with it. Its basic ingredients are zucchini, eggplant, tomatoes and onions, and you may vary the proportions and the seasonings as you please without affecting the essential tastefulness of the dish. You can use it as a main dish, or as the vegetable accompaniment to some simple meat dish.

# RATATOUILLE (*Vegetable Ragout*)

*4 tablespoons butter*
*4 tablespoons olive oil*
*3 medium onions, thinly sliced*
*2 green peppers, seeded and diced*
*2 medium eggplants, peeled and diced*
*5 tomatoes, peeled and diced*
*4 medium zucchini, sliced*
*Salt and pepper to taste*
*2 medium cloves garlic, pressed*
*½ teaspoon fines herbes (chives, chervil and thyme)*
*2 tablespoons chopped parsley*

Put butter and olive oil in stewpot over moderate heat and sauté onion until very light golden brown. Add peppers and eggplants, reducing heat, and cook 7 minutes, stirring frequently. Add the tomatoes and zucchini, cover tightly and simmer very gently for ½ hour. Add salt and pepper to taste, garlic and fines herbes, and continue cooking uncovered for 10 minutes. Stir in chopped parsley and cook another 5 minutes before serving. *Serves 6.*

# 7

## SPECIAL STEWS FOR GUESTS

STEWS are really great for feeding guests at dinner parties, although they are hardly ever identified as such. "Come share my stew" is what you say to your sister or the close friends with whom you take off your shoes and don't bother about a tie. Otherwise, it's "coq au vin" or "boeuf bourguignonne" or "curried lamb" or whatever. Which, perhaps, is as it should be. We all need a little elegance in our lives, and a stew by another name *may* (I don't say it *does*) taste better.

The beautiful thing about serving a stew is that it is so easy; stews are ideal dinner party dishes. For one thing, a stew can—and probably should—be prepared at least a day in advance, stored in the refrigerator (where all that nice marrying process occurs) and then reheated just before serving. This means that the hostess can be with her guests, where the action is, instead of in the kitchen, struggling over some recalcitrant delicacy, burning her fingers and losing her cool in the process.

Another advantage to stews is that you don't need a whole lot of other food in order to make a complete meal. Most stews are sufficient in themselves, needing only a tossed green salad, a loaf of bread and a bottle of wine for accessories. Some stews want rice or noodles in order to be well rounded, but these are easily prepared a short time before serving.

Stews are usually ample enough to give especially hungry guests a second helping, or, conversely, if your guests are the "think skinny" type, you can reheat the leftover stew for yourselves and have a private dinner party the next evening. (Use the money that you save to buy another bottle of wine.) I don't mean that you should scrape the leavings on the plates back into the stewpot—if your experience is the same as ours, there won't be anything left on the plates to be scraped.

Finally, a stew is easy to serve. If you have a pretty stewpot (and it's worth the investment), just put it on the table or serving board and let the guests serve themselves. If your stewpot's appearance does not measure up to its value, you will want to serve the stew from a preheated bowl. A nice touch is to warm the plates, too. Of course, in what some people wistfully refer to as the "good old days" (how good? and for whom?), the pot of stew was placed in the center of the table and everyone ate directly out of it, but I don't recommend going that far, although it would save a lot of dishwashing at the end of the meal.

All of the stews presented in this chapter have been often and successfully served at dinner parties in our home. I won't say they are the best of the book, but they are among the best, certainly. Together with the recipe for the main dish, I have given a suggested menu for the rest of the meal, but you will have to consult another cookbook for the recipes for these accessories. The menus are intended as guidelines, merely, to give you some idea of how best to set off your stew. I think that you can regard a separate vegetable as optional when you are serving stew, as the salad usually meets this requirement. Also, as a general rule, the dessert you offer following a stew should be light and frothy— a mere wisp of a dessert—so as not to overload the digestive system. It has been my experience that guests tend to overextend themselves when eating stew, and you don't want them to leave the dinner table feeling uncomfortable.

Altogether, I am sure you will find stews to be extremely popular dinner party fare.

*Dinner Party No. 1*

COQ AU VIN
WILD RICE
STEAMED BROCCOLI WITH BUTTER
TOSSED GREEN SALAD
HOT CROISSANTS AND BUTTER
RED WINE
COFFEE
CHERRIES JUBILEE

There are few dishes as elegant and exciting as coq au vin when it is properly prepared. In my opinion, the secret to a really top-notch version of this dish lies in two things: the use of salt pork and the flaming of the brandy. As is the case with most secrets, these are small but essential—like those little whatchamacallits without which your car wouldn't run. The following recipe yields 4 portions, and if you wish to serve more people, add more chicken (either a whole one, or those parts you like best), but don't double up on the other ingredients, except perhaps the mushrooms. Serve the same red wine that you use in preparing the stew.

## COQ AU VIN

½  pound salt pork, diced
8  shallots, sliced
1  teaspoon seasoned salt
1  fryer chicken, 3 to 3½ pounds, disjointed
½  pound mushrooms, sliced

1  large clove garlic, pressed
2  ounces brandy, warmed
2  cups good red burgundy wine
6  sprigs parsley
Tops of 2 celery stalks
10  peppercorns
1  bay leaf
2  tablespoons butter
2  tablespoons flour

Put diced salt pork in stewpot over moderate heat, and add shallots as soon as grease comes out of pork. Stir frequently over moderate heat until bits of pork are browned. Remove shallots and cracklings with a slotted spoon and reserve. Shake seasoned salt over chicken pieces and brown them in the hot fat. Add mushrooms and garlic and sauté a few minutes. Pour off any excess fat, and pour on the brandy. Light at once and shake pot vigorously until flame goes out. Return shallots and cracklings to pot, and add wine. Make a bouquet garni by tying up the parsley, celery tops, peppercorns and bay leaf loosely in a piece of cheesecloth, and drop this into pot. Cover tightly and simmer 50 minutes. Discard bouquet garni, and empty pot into a large bowl. Melt butter in pot and blend in flour, then slowly pour liquid from bowl into the flour mixture, stirring well and bringing to a simmer. Add pieces of chicken at the last, and simmer all together 5 minutes before serving. *Serves 4.*

### Dinner Party No. 2

CURRIED LAMB
SAFFRON RICE
CONDIMENTS: ground peanuts; chopped, hard-cooked

egg; shredded coconut; finely chopped onion; chopped raisins; peach or mango chutney; hot mustard

YOGHURT

SLICED TOMATOES

POPOVERS AND BUTTER

WHITE WINE

TEA

PRESERVED KUMQUATS

I got the following recipe for lamb curry from a Pakistani lady who was an excellent cook and a gracious hostess. She had nothing but contempt for American curry powder and American rice; the former she mixed herself, and the latter she had brought in from Pakistan. In addition to a liberal amount of curry powder (which was fairly powerful, the way she made it), she used dried chili peppers, with the result that an unsuspecting Westerner at one of her meals soon felt as though flames were coming out of his ears. I have toned down her recipe considerably.

To serve this curry, start with the saffron rice (made by adding a pinch or two of powdered saffron to the water in which the rice is cooked), add the curry and then sprinkle any or all of the condiments over the top. The yoghurt and the sliced tomato provide a very pleasant, cool, bland contrast to the spicy curry. Two types of bread are served in Pakistan: One is a flat, round bread, similar to a tortilla and called a chapati (you can buy this in some specialty shops, but it is frightfully expensive); the other is a puffed bread, to which the popover is the nearest American equivalent.

## CURRIED LAMB

4  tablespoons butter
2½  pounds boned, cubed lamb (removed from lamb shanks)

1 teaspoon seasoned salt
2 medium onions, chopped
1 clove garlic, pressed
1 large green pepper, seeded and chopped
2 stalks celery with leaves, chopped
¾ cup coconut milk (made by soaking shredded coconut in hot milk for about 1 hour)
1 cup chicken broth
½ cup sake or dry white wine
4 tablespoons curry powder
½ teaspoon powdered ginger
½ teaspoon turmeric
½ teaspoon paprika
¼ teaspoon cayenne pepper
¼ teaspoon ground cardamom
2 tablespoons flour
Olive oil
¼ cup seedless raisins
¾ cup yoghurt

Heat butter in stewpot over moderate heat, and sauté the cubes of salted lamb until brown on all sides. Remove meat to a platter and add onions, garlic, green pepper and celery to pot and sauté together for 10 minutes, stirring frequently. Add coconut milk, chicken broth and sake, and return meat to pot. Cover and simmer 1 hour. In a small bowl, mix together the curry powder, ginger, turmeric, paprika, cayenne pepper, cardamom and flour. Add just enough olive oil to make a thick paste. Drop this paste into pot by teaspoonfuls, stirring as you do so. Let simmer another ½ hour, or until meat is tender. Add raisins and simmer another 15 minutes. Stir in yoghurt just before serving. *Serves 6.*

SPICED POT ROAST
BUTTERED NOODLES
GREEN BEANS WITH BUTTER
LETTUCE AND TOMATO SALAD
HOT ROLLS AND BUTTER
RED BURGUNDY WINE
COFFEE
SHERBET

The following recipe was obtained from a neighbor of ours, a Bolivian lady of great charm, who served it to us for dinner one night and was thereafter hounded into imparting the instructions for making it. It is somewhat reminiscent of sauerbraten, but it is not marinated and therefore does not become impregnated with the tastes of wine and vinegar. In fact, the flavor of the spices is nicely muted, and the over-all effect is one of savoriness that your guests will find pleasantly different.

## SPICED POT ROAST

*2  tablespoons butter*
*1  tablespoon olive oil*
*1  3½- to 4-pound chuck roast*
*Salt and pepper*
*2  large onions, thinly sliced*
*1  bay leaf, crumbled*
*¼  cup water*
*¼  cup wine vinegar*
*¼  cup sake or dry white wine*
*1  tablespoon brown sugar*
*1  cinnamon stick*
*6  whole cloves*
*¼  teaspoon allspice*

*Water, if needed*
½  cup raisins
6  gingersnaps, crumbled

Put butter and olive oil in stewpot over medium heat.
Sprinkle roast with salt and pepper and brown on all
sides. Add onions, bay leaf, water, vinegar, sake and
brown sugar, and bring to gentle boil. Tie the cinnamon stick and whole cloves loosely in a piece of
cheesecloth, and add to pot with allspice. Cover and
simmer 2 hours, adding water if needed. Turn meat
over and add raisins, simmer another ½ hour or more,
until meat is tender. Just before serving, stir in crumbled gingersnaps and cook until sauce is thickened.
Remove roast to platter and slice, pouring hot sauce
over the slices. *Serves 6 to 8.*

## Dinner Party No. 4

VEAL SCALOPPINI
RISOTTO
STEAMED WHOLE ZUCCHINI, HALVED AND BUTTERED
ITALIAN OR FRENCH BREAD AND BUTTER
WHITE BURGUNDY WINE
COFFEE
BISCUIT TORTONI

There are many delightful stews to be made with veal,
but I think one of the nicest ways to serve it is in the
form of scaloppini stewed in wine. Scaloppini, or escalopes, are cut from the fillet and are very choice, small
portions. They should be cooked gently to retain their
tenderness, and served with the flourish they deserve,
garnished with parsley or watercress and/or a lemon
wedge. If you're feeling very Italian when you prepare
this dish, you can serve ravioli instead of risotto.

174.

# VEAL SCALOPPINI

*1 to 1½ pounds veal escalopes (1 inch thick)*
*¾ cup grated Romano cheese*
*Salt and pepper*
*3 tablespoons butter*
*½ cup bouillon*
*¼ cup sake or dry white wine*
*1 tablespoon lemon juice*
*1 clove garlic, pressed*
*½ teaspoon fines herbes (parsley, chives, chervil and thyme)*
*½ cup Marsala wine*

Lay the escalopes out flat on your cutting board and sprinkle them generously with grated cheese. Beat lightly with an empty milk bottle until cheese is beaten in. Turn the escalopes and pour more cheese over them and beat some more. Continue this process until all the cheese is mashed into the meat and the cutlets are about ¼ inch thick. Cut into slices 1 inch wide and sprinkle with salt and pepper. Heat butter in bottom of stewpot over medium high heat, drop in the slices of meat and brown quickly on both sides. Add bouillon, sake, lemon juice and garlic, and simmer 15 minutes. Add fines herbes and wine, and continue cooking another 15 minutes, or until meat is quite tender. *Serves 4.*

## Dinner Party No. 5

COMPANY BEEF STEW
TOSSED GREEN SALAD
HOT ROLLS AND BUTTER
RED WINE
COFFEE

### FRESH FRUIT SPRINKLED WITH GRAND MARNIER OR OTHER LIQUEUR

A writer/cook gave us the recipe for this stew, pointing out the unusual thickening agent (tapioca) used. We tried it and liked it, and pass it along to you herewith. Another unusual aspect to this stew is that it is cooked in the oven. You can cook it on top of the stove if you want to, but over the very lowest heat you can arrange, so that the stew barely simmers. A note of caution: Instant Tapioca tends to lose its powers after a month or so. Throw it out and get a new box every so often.

## COMPANY BEEF STEW

2 *pounds lean beef shoulder, cubed*
6 *medium carrots, sliced lengthwise*
3 *medium onions, chopped*
5 *stalks celery, sliced*
6 *medium potatoes, quartered*
1 *tablespoon Instant Tapioca*
1 *tablespoon sugar*
1 *teaspoon salt*
¼ *teaspoon black pepper*
1 *cup tomato juice*
1 *cup dry red wine*

Put all the ingredients together in a large casserole with a cover and cook in a 350° oven for 3 hours. Or you may bring them all to a very slow simmer in your stewpot, cover tightly and simmer 2 to 3 hours on top of the stove until meat is tender, adding a little water if needed. *Serves 4 to 6.*

BOEUF BOURGUIGNONNE
PLAIN BOILED RICE
TOSSED GREEN SALAD
FRENCH BREAD AND BUTTER
RED BURGUNDY WINE
COFFEE
CHOCOLATE PUDDING

Beef Burgundy is an excellent dinner party dish, yet relatively simple to prepare. You must let the beef cook a long time in the wine (it should barely bubble once in a while), and your meal is certain to win the praise of any guest who is lucky enough to be served it. That is, it will earn flattering remarks if you don't get chintzy in the matter of the wine. Use a good imported burgundy or equivalent domestic red wine, and you have it made. Let the stew cook along at its own slow speed while you talk with your guests, and, in due course, you will serve a pleasant, relaxed and delicious meal.

## BOEUF BOURGUIGNONNE (*Beef Burgundy*)

*3  tablespoons butter*
*4  medium onions, sliced*
*2½  pounds lean beef shoulder, cubed*
*2  tablespoons flour*
*1½  teaspoons seasoned salt*
*½  cup bouillon*
*¼  cup sake*
*1  cup good red burgundy*
*½  teaspoon fines herbes (parsley, chives, chervil and thyme)*
*1  pound mushrooms, sliced*

Heat butter in stewpot over moderate heat, and sauté

onions until light brown. Remove onions and reserve. Shake cubes of meat in a paper bag containing flour and seasoned salt, then brown in the remaining butter, adding butter if needed. Add bouillon, sake, burgundy and fines herbes, cover and simmer gently for 2 hours or until meat is just beginning to become tender. Add ½ water and ½ burgundy if more liquid is needed. Add mushrooms and simmer from ½ to 1 hour, or until meat is tender. *Serves 6.*

## *Dinner Party No. 7*

OLD-FASHIONED BEEF STEW
TOSSED GREEN SALAD
FRESH BREAD AND BUTTER
DRY RED WINE
COFFEE
FROSTED GRAPES

When you say "stew," most people think of something like the following: some kind of beef cooked in a thickened liquid together with several vegetables, usually potatoes, carrots and onions. And it is certainly true that this kind of stew is well nigh unbeatable for heartiness, flavor, aroma and economy. The fact that it is unpretentious and inexpensive does not mean it should be eschewed as dinner party fare. The following stew deserves the best batch of guests you can find. You'll be licking your lips just from reading the recipe.

## OLD-FASHIONED BEEF STEW

1  *cup vegetable oil*
2½  *pounds boned shoulder roast, cubed*
2  *medium onions, chopped*
4  *stalks celery, sliced*

18 small carrots, scraped
1 large clove garlic, pressed
1 teaspoon salt
1 teaspoon celery salt
1 teaspoon basil
½ teaspoon orégano
1 tablespoon paprika
¾ cup flour
2 cups red burgundy wine
2 cups water
4 cups bouillon
1 bay leaf
12 peppercorns
4 medium tomatoes, peeled and quartered
1 medium potato, quartered
12 small white onions, peeled and whole

Put oil in stewpot over medium high heat, and drop in
cubes of meat when oil is hot. Brown well on all sides,
then add onions, celery, carrots, garlic, salt and celery
salt. Sauté all together 10 minutes, stirring constantly.
Reduce heat to very low. Mix basil, orégano, paprika
and flour together, and shake into pot as you stir to
blend well. Then stir in burgundy, water and bouillon,
and bring to a gentle simmer. Tie bay leaf and peppercorns loosely in cheesecloth, add to pot with tomatoes
and simmer 1½ hours. Add potato and onions and cook
40 minutes or until meat is tender. *Serves 8.*

## Dinner Party No. 8

FLAMED POT ROAST
BUTTERED NOODLES
HOT ROLLS AND BUTTER
DRY RED WINE
COFFEE
PETIT FOURS

There was a time when pot roast was considered poverty fare, not fit for polite company. What with meat prices the way they are these days, pot roast is no more a poor man's dish than is any other form of beef. Furthermore, a pot roast can and should be a tender and succulent dinner dish which any hostess may be proud of serving. In the following recipe, the flaming may sound like unnecessary razzle-dazzle to you, but it really makes a difference, so don't skip it. Serve the same red wine that you use for cooking the pot roast.

## FLAMED POT ROAST

1  4-pound chuck roast
2  cloves garlic, cut in eighths lengthwise
2  tablespoons flour
1  teaspoon seasoned salt
5  tablespoons bacon drippings
5  tablespoons brandy or light rum
2  medium onions, sliced
5  medium carrots, sliced lengthwise
4  stalks celery with leaves, sliced
2  medium tomatoes, peeled and quartered
2  cups dry red wine
1  bay leaf, crumbled
1  teaspoon salt
½  teaspoon pepper
1  teaspoon fines herbes (parsley, chives, chervil and thyme)
1  pound mushrooms, sliced
Instant flour

With a small, sharp-pointed knife, cut slits on all sides of the roast and insert slivers of garlic as far as they can be pushed. Now pat in the flour mixed with seasoned salt on all sides. Heat bacon drippings quite hot in stewpot and brown meat on all sides. When well

180

browned, turn out fire and pour brandy or rum over the meat, lighting it immediately. Shake pot until flames goes out. Turn fire under pot to low, add onions, carrots, celery, tomatoes and wine. Bring to a gentle boil, add bay leaf, salt, pepper and fines herbes. Cover and simmer gently for about 3 hours, until meat is tender. Add mushrooms and cook 15 minutes. Remove from fire and let sit 5 minutes before shaking in instant flour while stirring to thicken sauce to desired consistency. *Serves 8.*

## Dinner Party No. 9

BEEF BLANQUETTE
NOODLE RING
LETTUCE AND TOMATO SALAD
WARM FRENCH BREAD AND BUTTER
RED WINE
COFFEE
BAVARIAN CREAM

A "blanquette" is simply a stew served with a white sauce. It can be made with veal, lamb, chicken or, as in this case, beef. It can be cooked in the white sauce, or the white sauce can be made and added just before serving. In this case, sour cream is the essential ingredient and gives the dish a nice tang, something akin to beef Stroganoff. You can make the blanquette the day before the party up to the point of cooking the noodles and adding the mushrooms, olives and sour cream. Then, about half an hour before serving, prepare the noodles and reheat the blanquette and finish it off. It makes a very nice party dish.

# BEEF BLANQUETTE

4  tablespoons flour
1½  teaspoons seasoned salt
2  pounds lean beef in 1-inch cubes
4  tablespoons butter
½  teaspoon nutmeg
1  bay leaf
1  cup water
18  small white onions, whole
½  pound button mushrooms, whole
½  cup stuffed green olives, sliced
1  cup sour cream

Put flour and seasoned salt in paper bag and shake beef cubes to coat well. Melt butter in stewpot over medium heat and brown meat on all sides. Add seasoned flour to absorb any excess fat. Add nutmeg, bay leaf and water, cover and simmer slowly for 1½ hours. Add onions and mushrooms and continue cooking 40 minutes, or until onions are tender. Add stuffed olives and sour cream, and stir until it begins to bubble. *Serves 6.*

## *Dinner Party No. 10*

LAMB RAGOUT
PLAIN BOILED RICE
SWEET CHUTNEY
HOT ROLLS AND BUTTER
RED WINE
COFFEE
FRESH FRUIT

This is a fun dish, because of all of the ingredients it contains. It is fun to shop for, fun to make and fun to serve. It has a nice spicy taste, because of the coriander and cumin, and you don't even have to serve a salad with it, in view of the many vegetables it contains. A sweet chutney sets it off perfectly.

## LAMB RAGOUT

*3 pounds boned shoulder of lamb in 1½-inch cubes*
*2 tablespoons flour*
*¼ teaspoon cayenne pepper*
*¼ teaspoon black pepper*
*2 teaspoons seasoned salt*
*¼ teaspoon paprika*
*¼ teaspoon saffron*
*1½ teaspoons coriander*
*½ teaspoon cumin*
*1 teaspoon sugar*
*5 tablespoons bacon drippings*
*1 large clove garlic, pressed*
*4 small turnips, sliced*
*2 medium carrots, sliced*
*6 medium onions, thinly sliced*
*1 green pepper, seeded and diced*
*1 cup tomato purée*
*3 tablespoons seeded raisins*
*Water, if needed*
*1 can black-eyed peas*

Dry cubes of meat between paper towels. Mix together flour, cayenne pepper, black pepper, seasoned salt, paprika, saffron, coriander, cumin and sugar. Roll each cube of meat in this mixture, then melt drippings in stewpot over medium heat, and brown the cubes on all sides. Remove browned meat and reserve. Add garlic, turnips, carrots, onions and green pepper to pot and sauté slowly for 10 minutes, stirring as you go. Add tomato purée and raisins, and return meat to pot. Simmer 2 hours, adding water if needed. Add peas and cook 10 minutes. *Serves 6 to 8.*

BOILED BEEF
PARSLEY POTATOES
COLD ZUCCHINI MARINATED IN FRENCH DRESSING
SOURDOUGH BREAD AND BUTTER
RED WINE
COFFEE
BRANDIED PEACHES

This is a good dinner party dish for those occasions when the budget simply will not stretch to encompass a standing rib roast. You boil—or, more correctly, simmer—the beef with all sorts of good things, and the result is a tender, tasty piece of meat that slices like a dream and will be especially appealing to the gentlemen present. I don't know why it is assumed that men's tastes in food are simpler than women's, and I am not sure that it is true. Anyhow, the men and the women will enjoy this dish, regardless of their relative degrees of sophistication.

## BOILED BEEF

4 to 5 pound rump roast
2½ quarts water
2 onions, halved
2 carrots, whole
1 stalk celery
¼ small head cabbage
2 small turnips, halved
½ teaspoon tarragon
½ teaspoon basil
½ teaspoon marjoram
12 peppercorns
2 whole cloves

¼ teaspoon allspice
1 teaspoon ground chicory (optional)

Put roast in stewpot with water and bring to a good boil, uncovered. If a scum appears, skim it off. Cover and simmer for 1½ hours. Add onions, carrots, celery, cabbage, turnips, tarragon, basil, marjoram, peppercorns, cloves, allspice and chicory (if desired). Simmer another 1½ hours, or until meat is very tender. Remove roast from pot, slice and serve with horseradish sauce. *Serves 8.*

## Dinner Party No. 12

BRAISED SIRLOIN OR TENDERLOIN TIPS
BOILED POTATOES WITH CHOPPED PARSLEY
ASPARAGUS SPEARS
HOT ROLLS AND BUTTER
TOSSED SALAD
RED WINE
COFFEE
APPLE PIE WITH CHEESE

Sirloin or tenderloin tips are not available at economy prices, but they cook into a beautiful stew and are rather elegant to serve at a dinner party. They are easy to prepare, too, so easy, in fact, that the local hash house may well be distinguished for its tenderloin tips. The important thing is the meat, for which there can be no substitutes.

## BRAISED SIRLOIN OR TENDERLOIN TIPS

3 tablespoons flour
1 teaspoon seasoned salt
2 pounds sirloin or tenderloin tips in 1½-inch cubes

185

*3 tablespoons butter*
*1 large onion, thinly sliced*
*1 cup beef bouillon*
*½ cup water*
*½ cup sake or dry white wine*
*2 teaspoons soy sauce*
*2 teaspoons chopped parsley*
*Instant flour, if needed*

Put flour and seasoned salt in paper bag and shake the cubes of meat in bag. Melt butter in stewpot over medium heat, and brown the cubes on all sides. Add onion and continue sautéing until golden brown. Add beef bouillon, water, sake, soy sauce and parsley, and simmer 45 minutes or more, depending on meat used. The sauce should be the correct consistency, but if thickening is needed, take off fire and let sit several minutes before shaking and stirring in instant flour as needed. *Serves 6.*

# 8

## JUST THE TWO OF US

*(Stews for Two)*

ON THE FACE of it, a stew for only two people seems a contradiction in terms. One thinks of a stew as a sort of synonym for ampleness. The stewpot sometimes resembles a caldron; a large ladle is used to serve up steaming portions; several pounds of meat and vegetables have gone into the savory broth; the minimum number of people required to polish off a stew at one sitting is twelve, and so on and so forth.

Now, hear this: It is possible to make a stew that will serve two people without anything left over!

Personally, I don't know why anyone would want to do this, as leftover stew is better than almost anything, except perhaps leftover spaghetti sauce. But if you are leaving on an extended trip tomorrow, or if you are only going to be where you are for one night, or if you are one of those tragic people who is constitutionally unable to face leftover anything, then this chapter is for you.

Preparing this chapter has taxed the ingenuity of both myself and my husband, for we are very much of the school which advocates making "a lot so that we can have some for tomorrow." It is extremely difficult for people of this persuasion to make a small stew. We always make a stew that is as large as the pot, and we nearly always use the largest pot we can find. Our stewpot is a splendid creation of enamel over cast iron and holds seven quarts; it was obviously not the vessel in which to prepare a stew for two. But test we must, so we used a small saucepan and practiced reducing quantities until we had a combination of ingredients that would fit so minuscule a pot. It was heartbreaking work, conducted to the accompaniment of a fair amount of grumbling, snide remarks and other displays indicating frustration of the artistic temperament.

Clearly, not everything stewable is capable of being compressed into a stew for two. One would be hard put to find a pot roast for two, or to make a bouillabaisse that will serve only two people. Similarly, a pot of chicken and dumplings must be on the large side, if only because it is not possible to make but four dumplings. I have, however, tried to give a representative assortment of stews cut to size, and hope that this chapter will be useful to people who have a need for tiny stews, inexplicable as that may be.


To BEGIN WITH, here is a basic beef stew that has been put through the reduction chamber. In this, as in all of the stews in this chapter, the assumption is that the two people involved have hearty appetites. (If your appetite does not respond to the tantalizing aroma of a stew, you had better consult your physician.) If you are not hungry, then this stew will probably serve three instead of two. But if you are *really* not hungry, you ought not to be tackling a stew in the first place.

### BASIC BEEF STEW FOR TWO

> 2 *tablespoons butter*
> ½ *pound beef shoulder, cubed*
> 1 *small onion, thinly sliced*
> 1 *cup hot water*
> ¼ *cup tomato juice*
> 1 *bay leaf*

*Salt and pepper to taste*
*4  small carrots, halved lengthwise*
*1  medium potato, quartered*
*Instant flour*

Melt butter in small pot over medium heat, and brown the cubes of beef lightly. Throw in onion and sauté until onion is golden and meat is golden brown. Add water, tomato juice, bay leaf, and salt and pepper to taste. Cover and simmer for 1½ hours. Remove bay leaf and add carrots and potato. Continue cooking for ½ hour. Turn off heat and let sit several minutes before stirring in instant flour to thicken sauce slightly. *Serves 2.*

LAMB STEW for two is just as feasible as a small stew with beef, and lamb is one of my favorite stew ingredients because the meat is so succulent. The following recipe is very simple as well as tasty, and you can use the other half of the package of beans as the vegetable for tomorrow night's meal.

## LAMB STEW FOR TWO

*2  lamb shanks*
*1  tablespoon flour*
*½  teaspoon seasoned salt*
*1½  tablespoons butter*
*1  medium onion, sliced*
*½  cup chicken broth*
*¼  cup hot water*
*1  medium tomato, peeled and quartered*
*½  package frozen baby green lima beans*
*¼  teaspoon orégano*

Trim all the meat carefully from lamb shanks, and cut into 1-inch cubes. Put flour and seasoned salt in paper bag and shake the pieces of meat to coat well. Melt butter in stewpot over medium heat and sear the pieces of lamb on all sides. Near the end, add onion and stir with meat until transparent. Add chicken broth, hot water and tomato, cover and reduce heat to a slow simmer. Cook 1 hour. Add lima beans and orégano, and simmer 20 minutes. *Serves 2.*

A BEEF STEW for two with a piquant flavor is the following, if the two of you are getting bored with just plain old stew. The wine vinegar, brown sugar and ginger give it such a lift that your appetite will be encouraged and you'll wish you had made enough stew for three or four instead of a tiny one for two.

## PIQUANT BEEF STEW FOR TWO

¾ *pound lean round steak*
1 *tablespoon butter*
2 *teaspoons flour*
½ *cup beef bouillon*
½ *cup water*
2 *tablespoons chopped onion*
½ *teaspoon salt*
¼ *teaspoon white pepper*
¼ *teaspoon ginger*
1 *tablespoon wine vinegar*
1 *tablespoon brown sugar*
1 *teaspoon Worcestershire sauce*

Cut meat into 1-inch pieces and brown on both sides in butter in bottom of stewpot. Remove pieces of meat and let butter become quite hot before shaking in the flour and blending. Reduce heat and let sit several minutes before stirring in bouillon and water. Return pieces of meat to pot, and add onion, salt, pepper, ginger, wine vinegar, brown sugar and Worcestershire sauce. Cover and simmer gently for 1 hour and 40 minutes, or until meat is tender. *Serves 2.*

IF YOU have never used nutmeg in your cooking, you have a great "discovery" in store, for nutmeg does marvelous things for simple dishes. I use it regularly on fried chicken; in fact, we describe our fried chicken as cooked with "tender, loving care and nutmeg." A tiny bit of nutmeg seems to emphasize the basic flavors present in the dish to which it is added; just be careful that you don't add too much or all of the basic flavors will be lost in the taste of nutmeg. The following recipe for pork chops uses nutmeg to advantage, and if you like it, you can start adding it to other foods as well.

## STEWED PORK CHOPS FOR TWO

2 *thick pork chops*
1 *tablespoon flour*
½ *teaspoon seasoned salt*
½ *medium onion, chopped*
2 *tablespoons sake or dry white wine*
2 *tablespoons water*
¼ *teaspoon nutmeg*

Trim all the fat from pork chops and put into stewpot over high heat. Fry the fat thoroughly until brown and crisp. Remove cracklings and reserve. Put flour and seasoned salt in paper bag and shake trimmed chops in it. Reduce heat to medium and brown the chops on both sides. Return cracklings to pot with onion, sake and water and simmer 30 minutes. Add nutmeg and continue cooking another 10 minutes or until chops are tender. *Serves 2.*

PORK CHOPS are easily stewed for just two people, as

the preceding recipe and the following one demonstrate. In fact, you could take any pork chop recipe in this book, cut the number of chops (keeping all other quantities the same), and create your own stew for two. This one is different in that it relies heavily on tomatoes as garnish.

## STEWED PORK CHOPS WITH TOMATOES
### FOR TWO

*3  pork chops, ½ inch thick*
*2  tablespoons butter*
*1  small onion, chopped*
*1  small green pepper, seeded and chopped*
*1  medium can tomatoes, drained*
*2  teaspoons Worcestershire sauce*
*Salt and pepper to taste*

Do not trim fat from chops. Melt butter in stewpot and brown chops on both sides. When second side is half cooked, add onion and green pepper. When chops are brown on both sides, add tomatoes, Worcestershire sauce, salt and pepper, cover and simmer very gently for 40 minutes, or until chops are tender. *Serves 2.*

ANOTHER cut of meat that can successfully be made into a stew for two is round steak. This is kept whole and simmered in a nicely seasoned sauce, and is likely to earn some well-deserved compliments from your partner at the dining table.

## STEWED ROUND STEAK FOR TWO

*2  tablespoons cooking oil*
*¾  pound round steak, ½ inch thick*
*2  tablespoons flour*
*½  cup good port wine*

½  cup beef bouillon
½  small onion, finely chopped
1  tablespoon brown sugar
½  teaspoon salt
½  teaspoon paprika
2  teaspoons lemon juice
1  tablespoon chopped parsley

Heat oil in stewpot over moderately high heat until hot but not smoking. Sear round steak on both sides and remove. Lower heat and stir in flour, then add port wine, bouillon and onion. Bring to a simmer, stirring well, then add brown sugar, salt, paprika and lemon juice. Drop meat back into pot and simmer 40 minutes. Add chopped parsley and cook another 20 minutes, or until meat is tender. *Serves 2.*

LIKE the round steak above, a veal cutlet can be stewed for two quite easily. In fact, all of these stews for two are so simple to make that even a novice or a husband can be certain to succeed with them. And, because they are stews, there won't be a huge stack of gritty pots and pans, spoons and forks for you to clean after the amateurs have left the premises. Just one small stewpot, and you can let that soak!

## STEWED VEAL CUTLET FOR TWO

1  tablespoon butter
¾  pound veal cutlet, ½ inch thick
1  small onion, finely chopped
4  tablespoons sake or dry white wine
4  tablespoons chicken broth
Salt and pepper to taste

Melt butter in stewpot over medium heat and brown the cutlet on both sides. Add onion and sauté until just soft. Add sake and chicken broth, and salt and pepper to taste. Cover and simmer very gently 45 minutes. *Serves 2.*

THE FACT that there are only two of you does not mean that you must forego serving a curry now and then. Following is a tasty curry of lamb which is modest both in size and in seasoning. If you like your curry to have a bit more bite to it, add more curry powder or a dash or two of turmeric. Serve this with rice (⅓ cup), either plain or colored with saffron.

## CURRIED LAMB FOR TWO

2 *lamb shanks*
1 *tablespoon flour*
¼ *teaspoon seasoned salt*
¼ *teaspoon orégano*
2 *tablespoons butter*
½ *cup chicken broth*
½ *cup water*
1 *medium onion, sliced*
½ *teaspoon curry powder*

Cut meat from shanks and cube into 1-inch pieces. Put flour, seasoned salt and orégano in paper bag, and shake cubes of meat in sack. Melt butter in stewpot over moderate heat and brown the pieces of lamb. Add chicken broth, water and onion, and simmer very slowly for 1½ hours. Stir in curry powder and cook another 10 minutes. *Serves 2.*

I AM SURE that everyone must know somebody who is able to make the most marvelous dinners for two out of odds and bits of things she happens to have handy. You or I might look in that good lady's refrigerator or pantry and see nothing that looked substantial enough for a meal, but she would concoct masterpieces as if by witchcraft. One such lady friend of mine presented me with a hamburger Stroganoff one evening, and I pass along her recipe to you impecunious twosomes who want just a little stew.

## HAMBURGER STROGANOFF FOR TWO

*1 tablespoon butter*
*½ pound ground shoulder meat*
*1 small onion, chopped*
*¼ pound mushrooms, thinly sliced*
*4 tablespoons sake or dry white wine*
*4 tablespoons water*
*Salt and pepper to taste*
*½ cup sour cream*

Melt butter in stewpot over medium heat, add ground meat and mash out with two-tined fork to separate the meat, and stir as you sauté it for 10 minutes. Add onion and mushrooms and stir them in as you cook another 10 minutes. Add sake and water, and salt and pepper to taste. Simmer 15 minutes, and add sour cream just before serving. *Serves 2.*

THE CHAPTER following this one is devoted to stewing leftovers, but this one is specifically measured out to serve two people, and here it is—a perfect way to dispose of the roast beef from Saturday's dinner party.

## LEFTOVER BEEF STEW FOR TWO

*1 tablespoon flour*
*½ teaspoon seasoned salt*
*1½ cups cooked beef, cubed*
*2 tablespoons bacon drippings*

1 small onion, sliced
1 clove garlic, whole
½ cup bouillon
½ cup water
¼ cup sake or dry white wine
1 medium potato, cubed
2 medium carrots, halved lengthwise

Put flour and salt in paper bag and shake cubes of meat to coat well. Melt drippings in stewpot over moderate heat, and brown the cubes. Add onion and whole garlic at the last and sauté 5 minutes. Add bouillon, water, sake, potato and carrots, and simmer 30 minutes, or until carrots are tender. Remove clove of garlic before serving. *Serves 2.*

PURISTS in the matter of sea food will look down their noses at the following recipe for New England clam chowder, because it uses canned clams. But if you were to insist on using fresh clams in a stew for two, you would need only about half a dozen, which seems ridiculous. Anyhow, this chowder is delectable as it stands and is just right for two.

## NEW ENGLAND CLAM CHOWDER FOR TWO

2 slices fat bacon, diced
1 medium onion, sliced
1 small potato, diced
1 6-ounce can minced clams
½ cup sake or dry white wine
¼ cup water
½ cup light cream
Salt and pepper to taste
1 shake Tabasco sauce

Lightly brown diced bacon in small stewpot, add onion

and sauté until onion is transparent. Add potato, juice from can of clams, sake and water. Cover and simmer 30 minutes. Add minced clams and cream, salt and pepper to taste and Tabasco sauce. Simmer gently for 2 minutes before serving. *Serves 2.*

# 9

## ODDS AND ENDS

### (Stewing Leftovers)

STEWS make such marvelous leftovers that, at first glance, it seems unnecessary to talk about making leftovers into stews. But I think many of us make stews out of leftovers without realizing that that is what we are doing. That bit of leftover roast beef or leg of lamb just naturally makes itself into a stew with the cook's hardly knowing what she is about. It's the stew made of leftovers that gets shunted into the last car on the train; it is never talked about, written down or exploited in any way. And that is a pity, really, because some mighty fine stews are made with leftovers, as any conscientious cook knows full well.

There are people who refuse to eat leftovers. I know not why, but I suspect this prejudice dates back to days when iceboxes ran out of ice and food spoiled much more quickly and often than it does now in our modern refrigerators. (We once lived in an all-electric house, and every time there was a storm, lo! we were unable to cook, read, keep warm or put ice in our drinks for hours.) Also, it is true that a gray, greasy slice of pot roast is unappetizing, no matter how enthusiastic one may be about leftovers.

A friend of mine makes what I would call stews out of leftovers, but she calls them, instead, "supremes." Her family is served ham supreme, chicken supreme, veal supreme, beef supreme and so forth, and I think they are all much happier with leftovers for the fancy disguises that they wear.

A leftover needs to be disguised. A certain amount of the roast beef, the ham and the lamb can be sliced for sandwiches or to be served cold, but that still leaves a quantity of bits and pieces that are too small and irregular for slicing and too abundant and full of food value to be thrown away. The ideal solution for such odds and ends is the stew, and if you have some gravy left over, too, toss it in for extra flavor.

A stew made with leftovers is probably a more genuine creation than a stew made with fresh ingredients, because the cook necessarily is inventive in utilizing the resources at hand to the best advantage. This is the reason so few stews made with leftovers find their way into cookbooks; each such stew is a thing unto itself and is hardly ever written down.

In this chapter, I have written down some of the things that are done with leftovers at my house. In my opinion, they are stews—and mighty good ones, at that!

ONE OF the favorite stews at our house starts with roast beef bones, which are cooked for half a day in water with various seasonings in it. This gets the good out of the bones and loosens any meat that might still be attached to them. Then you cut up the leftover roast beef and, using the liquid in which the bones were cooked, you invent a stew that really deserves to be called "supreme." It is hard to duplicate such a stew when starting from scratch because it's the leftover roast beef bones that make it so good. And if you start with fresh bones (i.e., bones that have never been cooked), you must cook them for 10 to 12 hours to get the good out of them. Anyhow, here's a stew made with bones and bits of meat that will really be a treat for your family.

# LEFTOVER ROAST BEEF STEW

*Leftover standing rib roast*
3  *cups water*
1  *package dry onion soup mix*
1  *clove garlic, pressed*
2  *onions, sliced*
4  *stalks celery, chopped*
2  *tablespoons barley*
8  *medium carrots, halved lengthwise*
3  *potatoes, sliced*

Cut all bite-size bits of meat from bones and reserve. Put bones in stewpot with water and bring to boil. Add onion soup mix, garlic, onions, celery and barley, cover and simmer for 2 hours or more, until all the gristle slides easily from the bones. Remove bones from liquid and cool so they can be cleaned thoroughly. Return bits to pot with any meat you have saved from the beginning, add carrots and potatoes and cook 30 minutes, or until vegetables are tender. *Serves 4.*

SOMEBODY once had a real inspiration as to what to do with leftovers and invented "jambalaya," a wonderful Creole dish that every homemaker should have in her repertoire. It calls for ham and turkey or ham and chicken and comes in especially handy during the Christmas holiday season when large gatherings of friends and family devour most but not all of the baked ham and the roast turkey. Mix the two leftovers together and serve a jambalaya that will make the entire family applaud.

# JAMBALAYA

3 tablespoons butter
2 onions, finely chopped
1 clove garlic, pressed
1 cup diced cooked turkey
1 cup diced cooked ham
1 teaspoon salt
½ teaspoon black pepper
1 cup raw rice
4 cups chicken broth
1 green pepper, seeded and diced
1 cup canned tomatoes, drained
½ cup sake or dry white wine

Melt butter in stewpot over medium heat, add onions and garlic and sauté until onions are tender. Add turkey and ham and sauté together for 5 minutes. Add salt, pepper and rice, and continue cooking, stirring frequently, until rice is very light brown. Add chicken broth, green pepper and tomatoes, cover and simmer 30 minutes, or until rice is cooked. Add sake and cook another 5 minutes. *Serves 4.*

ONCE UPON A TIME, my husband and I decided that we would go out to dinner on Monday (or maybe it was Tuesday), and, consequently, did not do any marketing that day. Comes the time for proceeding to the restaurant of our choice, and it was raining and cold and generally hostile to our intentions. We decided that only idiots would go out in such weather, and, as we did not wish to be so classified, we stayed home. But then arose the problem of what to eat. An investigation of the refrigerator disclosed that all we had of any substance was a fair-size piece of steak and two moderate slices of baby beef liver, already cooked. So we did just what you would do, too: we made a stew. It was so good that now we plan our meals so as to acquire the requisite leftovers for a steak and liver stew.

## LEFTOVER STEAK AND LIVER STEW

*2 tablespoons butter*
*3 onions, sliced*
*½ clove garlic, pressed*
*4 sausage links*
*½ teaspoon seasoned salt*
*Flour*
*Sake and water in equal parts*
*½ pound cooked steak, cubed*
*3 slices cooked liver, cubed*

Melt butter in stewpot over low heat, add onions and garlic and sauté 10 minutes. Add sausage links and seasoned salt and continue cooking 10 minutes. Shake in enough flour to absorb all the grease, and continue cooking over low heat while stirring in equal parts of sake and water to make a thin sauce. Add cubed steak and simmer gently 10 minutes before adding cubed liver. Heat the liver thoroughly before serving. *Serves 2 or 3.*

CHICKEN does not present as great a disposal problem as do other meat dishes, as there is nearly always somebody around who will chew on the thigh or the back or the wishbone or whatever, and soon all that is left is a very bare carcass. There are times, however, when there is enough chicken or turkey left to make a stew a reasonable project, particularly if your family is partial to white or dark meat and eschews the other. You can feed them what they think they don't like in the form of a stew, and they will praise you for it.

# LEFTOVER CHICKEN STEW

*1½ to 2 cups boned leftover cooked chicken*
*3  tablespoons flour*
*1  teaspoon seasoned salt*
*4  tablespoons butter*
*Milk*
*Chicken broth*
*1  package green onion dip mix*
*1  small can pimientos, diced*
*1  small can sliced mushrooms*

Cube leftover chicken across the grain and shake in
paper bag containing flour and seasoned salt. Melt butter in stewpot over low heat, lift pieces of floured
chicken from sack in fingers to shake off excess flour,
and drop them in the hot butter to brown lightly. Slowly add enough milk to form a thick paste over low heat,
then stir in chicken broth to make a thin sauce. Add
green onion mix, pimientos and mushrooms, and simmer very slowly for 30 minutes. *Serves 4.*

IF YOU really want to go the whole route with your leftover chicken, then the following recipe is for you. You
start with what you have left of a roast chicken, as-
suming that there is a cup or two of meat involved, and
use the whole thing, including the carcass. In fact, the
bones are what make this stew one to be remembered,
for you cook out all of the good flavor of the bones
that did not get cooked away in the roasting process,
and you'd be surprised at how much there is.

## LEFTOVER ROAST CHICKEN STEW

*Chicken bones and carcass*
*1  to 2 cups leftover cooked chicken*
*3  cups water*

1 package chicken noodle soup mix
4 tablespoons raw rice
1 green pepper, seeded and diced
2 stalks celery, diced with leaves
8 small white onions, whole

To do this properly, you should save all the leg and wing bones after the meat has been sliced from them for serving. Cut all bite-size pieces of chicken from bones and carcass and reserve with any other leftover chicken meat. Put all the bones in a stewpot with water and bring to boil. Add chicken soup mix, and then rice, green pepper and celery. Cover and simmer very slowly for 1½ hours. Remove all bones from pot and let cool so any bits of goodness adhering to them can be easily removed. Add onions and continue cooking 30 minutes. Add all bits of chicken to pot and cook another 10 minutes. *Serves 4.*

UNLIKE my friend who called her leftover creations "supremes," I call mine "inventions," which is an indication of how far afield I go sometimes to make something out of nothing. An invention is fun to make because you have no idea at the beginning what will come out of the pot at dinnertime, except that it will taste good, because almost any tactful combination of tasty ingredients will result in something edible. I say "tactful" because, of course, it is possible to put together ingredients which, by themselves, are perfectly good, but which do not make good companions. Your own sense of taste has to tell you whether the items you are dealing with will get along well together.

## LEFTOVER CHICKEN INVENTION

2 tablespoons butter
1 onion, sliced

2  *tablespoons flour*
*1½  cups chicken broth*
*½  cup sake or dry white wine*
*1½  cups diced, cooked chicken*
*1  2-ounce jar stuffed green olives*
*1  2½-ounce jar sliced mushrooms*

Melt butter in pot. Add onion and cook until transparent. Then sprinkle flour into butter and stir until a smooth paste is formed. Add chicken broth and sake, a little at a time, to make a smooth sauce. Add chicken, olives and mushrooms. Cook for ½ hour and serve over rice. *Serves 6.*

FOR THE PURPOSES of this cookbook, I wrote down some of my better "inventions" as I was doing them, and my notes from these occasions are spattered with butter and oniony fingerprints. I should point out that the ingredients of these dishes are there because they just happened to be on hand on the day in question. For example, I use ripe olives and stuffed green olives interchangeably, despite the wide difference in flavor, depending upon what is available in my cupboard. Similarly, I always use fresh mushrooms in preference to canned, if I happen to have them on hand. Even mushroom stems are preferable to canned mushrooms. Canned mushrooms are so expensive that I save them to serve on toothpicks at parties.

## LEFTOVER LAMB INVENTION

*2  tablespoons butter*
*2  small onions, sliced*
*3  shallots, minced*
*1  cup fresh mushrooms, sliced*
*2  tablespoons flour*
*1  cup chicken broth*

1½ to 2 cups cooked leg of lamb, diced
10 to 12 ripe olives, sliced
¼ cup slivered almonds
1 package frozen peas

Melt butter in stewpot and cook onions, shallots and mushrooms until tender. Sprinkle flour over all to make a paste. Add chicken broth gradually, stirring constantly, until thoroughly blended. Add lamb, olives and almonds. Bring to a boil and then reduce heat to slow simmer. Cover pan and cook for ½ hour. Add frozen peas, breaking them apart with a fork, and cook until peas are tender. This makes a fairly thick stew that needs no other accompaniment, although noodles are good with it. *Serves 6 to 8.*

LEFTOVER pot roast makes scrumptious sandwiches, but if you have no need for sandwiches or are bored with them, then a stew is a great way of disposing of the pot roast remains. The quantities given in these recipes for leftovers, by the way, do not have to be strictly adhered to. If your canned mushrooms hold 4 ounces instead of 2½, use all of the mushrooms in the can, unless you want to serve them as hors d'oeuvres or something. The marvelous thing about cooking leftovers is the amount of latitude you are allowed in terms of adding and subtracting. That's what makes these dishes real "inventions." Now that you know how, you can invent a few of your own.

## LEFTOVER POT ROAST INVENTION

2 tablespoons butter
¼ cup chopped celery
1 medium onion, chopped
1 can condensed mushroom soup
1 can water

1½  cups leftover pot roast, cut in 1-inch cubes
1  cup elbow macaroni

Melt butter in large, heavy pan. Add celery and onion and cook until tender. Add mushroom soup and water slowly, so as to blend evenly. Add pot roast cubes and bring mixture to a boil. Add macaroni a little at a time so that the liquid continues to boil. Reduce heat to slow simmer and cook for ½ hour or until macaroni is tender. *Serves 6 to 8.*

POT ROAST is one of the more difficult food items to dispose of when it is left over. Reheating tends to dry out, and a good part of the roast near the bone is not susceptible to being sliced for sandwiches. But a left over pork roast can be stewed in much the same way as leftover lamb or beef. The following is an invention of my husband's, who gets exasperated with pork roasts because they are so hard to carve.

## LEFTOVER PORK ROAST STEW

1 to 2 cups leftover cooked pork roast
Bones from pork loin roast
2  cups chicken broth
1  cup water
1  tablespoon soy sauce
Salt and pepper to taste
1  apple, peeled, cored and quartered
1  tomato, peeled and quartered
¼  cup raisins
1  cup sliced mushrooms
Instant flour

Hack off all the meat you can from the bones in bite-size pieces and reserve. Put bones, chicken broth, water and soy sauce in stewpot and bring to a simmer. Add salt and pepper to taste. Simmer 1½ hours. Remove bones and set aside to cool. Add apple, tomato, raisins and mushrooms. Cook 30 minutes. Remove all bits of goodness from the bones and add to any leftover pork from roast cut in bite-size pieces. Simmer another 10 minutes. Turn off heat for several minutes before adding instant flour to make a sauce of the desired consistency. *Serves 6.*

ONE OF THE BEST leftover stews is, of course, the curry. As pointed out in previous sections of this book, you can curry almost anything, and that includes anything left over. This particular curry uses lamb, but you could substitute cooked chicken, beef, pork or veal. A curry is always an exciting dish to serve, and your family should welcome this method of utilizing a leftover. Serve it with saffron rice and a sweet-and-sour chutney (you can buy this ready-made, but it is also easy to make yourself), and spouse and children won't even know you're feeding them a leftover.

## LEFTOVER LAMB CURRY

*Leftover leg of lamb*
*1 cup coconut milk*
*1 cup water*
*1 clove garlic*
*2 medium onions, sliced*
*2 cups cubed cooked lamb*
*2 teaspoons curry powder*
*1 teaspoon salt*
*2 whole cloves*
*½ teaspoon ginger*
*½ teaspoon turmeric*
*½ teaspoon cumin*
*1 teaspoon coriander*

¼  teaspoon cayenne pepper
1  cup dried prunes

Trim any bite-size bits of meat from lamb bone, and disjoint. Make coconut milk by pouring 1 cup boiling water over ½ pound shredded coconut and letting stand 5 minutes. Press milk out through a sieve and put in stewpot with bone and water. Add garlic and onions, and simmer 1½ hours. Remove bone to cool. Add cooked lamb, curry powder, salt, cloves, ginger, turmeric, cumin, coriander, cayenne pepper and prunes. Simmer 30 minutes, or until prunes are soft. When bone is cooled, strip off any bits of gristle and meat and add to pot. *Serves 4.*

# INDEX

218

# Variety Cookbooks

Dine like a king at home! Unbelievably priced for everyone's pocket. Easy to read and follow directions. Recipes for simple to gourmet taste buds.

- ☐ **Budget Cooking for Four**
  **$2.00 Dinners For Four**
- ☐ **The Buffet Cookbook**
- ☐ **Chinese Cooking with American Meals**
- ☐ **Cooking With Eggs**
- ☐ **The New Hamburger Cookbook**
- ☐ **The New Hotdog Cookbook**
- ☐ **The Practical Fondue Cookbook**
- ☐ **The Quick & Easy Cookbook**
- ☐ **Savory Stews**
- ☐ **The Seafood Cookbook**

# ENCORE ROMANCES